Handwriting Without Tears®
Kindergarten
Teacher's Guide

Guide to Multisensory
Lessons and Activities for...

Handwriting Without Tears®

Name:

Print Child's Name

Letters and Numbers
For Me

cow   dog   kite   fish

by Jan Z. Olsen, OTR and Emily F. Knapton, OTR/L

Handwriting Without Tears®

Jan Z. Olsen, OTR

8001 MacArthur Blvd
Cabin John, MD 20818
301.263.2700
www.hwtears.com

Authors: Jan Z. Olsen, OTR and Emily F. Knapton, OTR/L
Illustrator: Jan Z. Olsen, OTR
HWT Graphic Designers: Leah Connor and Julie Koborg

The Handwriting Without Tears® program and teachers' guides are intuitive and packed with resources and information. Nevertheless, we are constantly developing new ideas and content that make handwriting easier to teach and to learn.

To make this information available to you, we created a password protected section of our website exclusively for users of this teacher's guide. Here you'll find new tips, in-depth information about topics described in this guide, extra practice sheets, other instructional resources, and material you can share with students, parents, and other educators.

Just go to **www.hwtears.com/click** and enter your passcode, **TGLN8**.

Enjoy the internet resources, and send us any input that you think would be helpful to others: janolsen@hwtears.com.

WELCOME

The Handwriting Without Tears® program continues to evolve. This *Kindergarten Teacher's Guide* is the culmination of successes from previous editions, plus many new ideas from our collaborations with teachers, occupational therapists, and administrators across the country.

We appreciate all the educators who bring such drive and curiosity to making handwriting easier for children. Your feedback and ideas have helped shape this guide.

Good handwriting is one of the foundation skills of language development. It is also a skill that regularly goes on public display and one of the first observable measures of school success. With your guidance, handwriting will be an easy victory for children, enabling them to do better in school.

You can help children develop their handwriting skills so they can focus on content rather than on the mechanics of letter and number formation. As children gain handwriting mastery, their writing becomes more fluid and automatic so they can write with speed and ease in all of their classes.

If you are in a hurry, jump straight to the lesson plans for *Letters and Numbers for Me*, starting on page 74 of this guide. When you have time, there is a wealth of information in the earlier sections that will give you new tools and insights into the handwriting process. Plus, you will learn about the multisensory techniques and products that engage children and delight teachers. As you get further along and see this icon for A Click Away, be sure to visit **www.hwtears.com/click** for more program information and resources.

Please keep the suggestions coming. Your comments, criticisms, and compliments help us learn what we can do to make the Handwriting Without Tears® program work even better for students and educators.

Thanks,

Jan Z. Olsen   *Emily F. Knapton*

Jan Z. Olsen, OTR   Emily F. Knapton, OTR/L

INTRODUCTION

Kindergarten Teacher's Guide is the guide to the student workbook, *Letters and Numbers for Me*. The tips and lesson plans here will help you be a great handwriting teacher. In addition to teaching posture, paper, and pencil skills, you will also teach:

- Letter skills
- Word skills
- Sentence skills

With each step, your students will easily learn what they needed to excel not only in the skill of handwriting, but also in the ability to assess their own handwriting skills. Our goal is to help students learn proper handwriting habits and then apply those habits naturally and automatically to all writing experiences.

Pay particular attention to the stages of learning:

1. Imitation (writing after a live demonstration)
2. Copying (writing from a model)
3. Independent Writing (writing without any assistance or models)

You will be amazed by what your students will learn when these skill levels are combined in well-coordinated instruction.

GETTING STARTED
Prepare

The Handwriting Process

Get Ready for Readiness

HANDWRITING INSTRUCTION
Choose Your Approach

Multisensory Lessons...29-59

Music and Movement...30

Wood Pieces Set...32

Mat Man™...44

Wet–Dry–Try...46

Door Tracing...50

Imaginary Writing...52

Letter Size and Place...54

Voices...55

Mystery Letters...56

Letter Stories...58

HANDWRITING WITHOUT TEARS

Eager to start?
Lessons start here.

Handwriting Without Tears®

Name:
Print Child's Name

Letters and Numbers For Me

cow dog kite fish

Need a schedule?
Guidelines are here.

GETTING STARTED
Prepare
ABOUT KINDERGARTEN WRITERS

Times are changing. Today's kindergarteners are expected to write more than ever. It's not uncommon for them to be expected to write in a journal in the first week of school. They need strong handwriting skills to meet these high expectations.

But what about your kindergarteners? They come from different home and preschool experiences. Some have just turned five, and others are nearly six. With early and late bloomers, with different English language skills, with advantaged and challenged children, you probably have quite a mix. As you get to know your students' skills, this guide will help you bring along those who are not as well prepared, fill in any missing skills for well prepared children, and develop all as capable writers. At the start of the year, you may observe reversals, awkward pencil grips, and writing from the bottom. Don't worry. Students may come to your class with handwriting problems, but you can help.

PREP YOUR SPACE...

Look at your kindergarten classroom. Do you have one of those modern classrooms with cafe style seating? Move those chairs and desks for handwriting lessons because children need to face the teacher to see the demonstration at the board or easel. When children face you, they hear more clearly. Ears are shaped to catch sound from the direction they face. This is so simple and amazing. Look at your class. If students are looking at you, they will see, hear, and pay closer attention.

Can all your students see you?

For Kindergarten Children

They come in all sizes. What about your furniture? Do the chairs, tables, and desks fit the children? The right size and style chair and desk affect school performance. One size chair will not fit every child. Check that every child can sit with feet flat on the floor and arms resting comfortably on the desk.

Having children face you during instruction, and having children sit in the right size furniture will give your instruction and their learning an immediate boost. Now let's get your room and supplies ready for handwriting lessons.

For Demonstrations

Double Line Chart Tablet
Demonstrate on this Double Line Chart. Children can practice on it too.

Print Wall Cards
Display the alphabet above the board to help children remember letters.

Name Cards
Give each child a place in the room. Model their name in capitals and title case.

For Multisensory Lessons

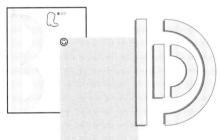

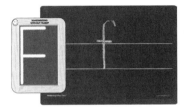

Slate & Blackboard with Double Lines
Use the Slate to teach capitals and numbers. The Blackboard with Double Lines is used to teach lowercase letters.

***Rock, Rap, Tap & Learn* CD**
Use the CD to make learning letters and numbers fun and memorable.

Wood Pieces Set, Capital Letter Cards & Mat
Use these readiness materials to develop skills in a playful but carefully structured way. The Mat and Cards use a ☺ as an orientation icon for the Wood Pieces.

Magic C Bunny
Make the puppet your teaching assistant. Your students can use him too.

For the Children

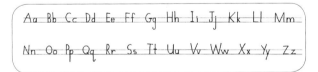

Print Alphabet Desk Strip
Adhere these stickers to a child's desk. They help children visually recall letters.

***Letters and Numbers for Me* Workbook**
Follow the lessons in the workbook. It's loaded with capital, lowercase, and number practice. Your students will love the fun activities, which develop their word, sentence, and paragraph skills.

FLIP Crayons™
Flip Crayons help children develop hand coordination and fine motor skills.

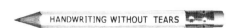

Pencils for Little Hands
Use golf-size pencils with children. Let them write with pencils that fit their hands.

The Handwriting Process

THE INTENT TO PREVENT

Good handwriting skills result from your thoughtful attention and instruction. Students require deliberate instruction to develop good habits and overcome bad ones.

With this guide and HWT materials, you will be prepared to help students make writing a natural and automatic skill. You'll find that their handwriting abilities and habits vary. Regardless of where they start, you can help them develop and improve their skills:

Teach	**Fix**
How to hold the pencil correctly	Awkward pencil grips

| Letters/numbers that face the right way | Reversals |

| Letters/numbers that start at the top | Starting at the bottom |

| Letters/numbers that are formed correctly and consistently | Incorrect letter/number |

PRINTING SKILLS FOR SPEED AND LEGIBILITY

You want children to write with speed and neatness while thinking about the content of their work. Would you like to know the secret of developing speed and legibility? Some people think it's practice, practice, practice that promotes speed. But practicing letters over and over actually makes them progressively messier. Some think that trying hard is what makes printing neat. But trying hard won't work unless children have been taught properly.

The secret to achieving speed and legibility is following the simple strategies in the HWT workbooks, guides, and multisensory products. The HWT program develops eight key skills:

Memory   Name letters and numbers quickly from a random list.
Visualize a letter or number quickly without seeing it.

Orientation   Print all letters and numbers without reversals.

Placement   Follow lines and place letters and numbers correctly on the baseline.

Size   Write in an appropriate size for kindergarten.
Make letters a consistent size.

Start   Start all letters and numbers at the top (except **d** and **e**).

Sequence   Make the letter parts in the correct order and direction.
Make the letter parts the same correct way every time.

Control   Print the letter parts neatly—no gaps, overlaps, or extra tracings.
Keep curved parts curved, straight parts straight, pointed parts pointed, etc.

Spacing   Keep letters in words close.
Leave space between words in sentences.

It is clear that each of these skills is important. Children who immediately know their letters or numbers and which way they face (Memory and Orientation) don't have to stop and think. They can write quickly. Children who make their letters sit correctly on the baseline and who make them a consistent size (Placement and Size) produce neat papers. Children who always start in the right place, and make the strokes the same way every time (Start and Sequence) are able to write quickly and neatly without thinking. (Control) will come naturally as children master the above skills. (Spacing) develops from good instruction and from using the worksheets and workbooks that provide enough room to write.

Speed and Neatness

Music teachers know about speed. It's the last thing they teach. First come the notes, rhythm, fingering or bowing, and finally, practice to reach an automatic, natural level. Then pick up the tempo! It's the same with handwriting. Take a lesson from a music teacher! Work on everything else and speed will come. Children who use poor habits are doomed to be slow or sloppy. Children with good habits can be both fast and neat. That's where we are heading.

DEVELOPMENTAL TEACHING ORDER

The HWT teaching order is planned to help children learn handwriting skills in the easiest, most efficient way. It's also planned developmentally to start with a review of the easy letters: the capitals. They are the first letters children learn. Your kindergarteners may know them, but you want to be sure they print them correctly. The capital teaching order will help you teach:

1. Correct formation: All capitals start at the top. Strokes are made in the correct sequence.
2. Correct orientation: No reversals.

To do this, start by teaching letters in groups on Gray Blocks.

Frog Jump Capitals

F E D P B R N M

These letters start at the top left corner with a big line on the left. When the first line is on the left, the next part is on the right side. This prevents reversals, while teaching good stroke habits.

Starting Corner Capitals

H K L U V W X Y Z

Reviewing these letters ensures that children start at the top left and use the left-to-right formation habit. Printing follows the same order as reading: top-to-bottom and left-to-right. This group promotes that habit.

Center Starters

C O Q G S A I T J

C O Q G start with a Magic C stroke. The good habits children learn here with **C O S T J** will make learning **c o s t j** much easier. There will be no problems with stroke direction or reversals.

The lowercase teaching order promotes similar success:

1. Good habits for letter formation: All lowercase letters (except **d** and **e**) begin at the top.
2. Correct placement: The tall, small, and descending letters are in proportion and placed correctly.
3. Correct orientation: No **b** – **d** confusion, no **g** – **q** confusion, no reversed letters!

To do this, the letters are taught in these groups:

c o s v w   t

The first five letters are exactly like their capitals, but just smaller. What an easy start! Just bring your good habits from capitals. Lowercase **t** is made like **T**, it's just crossed lower.

a d g

These high frequency letters begin with the familiar Magic c. Starting with **c** placed correctly helps children make and place the **d** tall and **g** descending.

u i e l k y j

Here are the rest of the vowels: **u i e**. Letters **u k y j** are familiar from capitals. The focus will be on careful placement and size.

p r n m h b

They dive! They start with the same pattern: dive down, swim up, swim over! We avoid **b** – **d** confusion by separating the letters and teaching them in different groups.

f q x z

Finally **f**! Letter **f** has a tricky start. Letter **q** is taught here to avoid **g** – **q** confusion. Letters **x** and **z** are familiar, but infrequently used.

INTEGRATION: HANDWRITING AND READING

Reading and handwriting share the same symbols—the letters of the alphabet—but they require very different skills and mastery processes. Understanding these differences helps you teach both subjects well and illustrates the importance of the letter teaching order for each.

Decoding for Reading and Encoding for Handwriting

Decoding requires deciphering printed words by identifying the sounds created by the letter symbols that combine to make the word. Lessons should be focused on visual and auditory skills. The teaching order for reading uses word building to develop and reinforce decoding skills. After children master the easier sounds, they are ready to move on to the sounds that are more difficult.

Encoding requires hearing spoken language and translating sounds into letter symbols. Handwriting also requires cognitive, motor, and visual recall skills. Therefore, the lessons should be multisensory. Imitating and copying help cement letter formation habits. The HWT letter teaching order supports the development of these skills because letters are taught in groups based on similarity of formation. After children master the easier letters, they are ready to move on to letters that are more difficult to form. Teaching handwriting and reading successfully at the same time is easy, but you need to be aware of the differences.

The handwriting and reading integration options shown below work best because they adhere to the fundamental principles of each discipline and incorporate lesson work from each in a way that fully supports skill development. Find the one that works best for you.

1. Separate the handwriting and reading teaching orders
Teach both programs in the recommended orders. Keep instruction separate until familiar letters appear. Then remind children of letters they know from handwriting or reading instruction.
- During handwriting, remember reading.
  Remind students of the previously learned letter sounds.
- During reading, remember handwriting.
  Remind students how to write letters that were previously taught.

A Click Away hwtears.com/click

2. Integrate the handwriting and reading teaching orders
Teach both programs in the recommended order, but supplement the particular letter lesson by teaching the basic lesson associated with the other discipline.
- During handwriting, integrate reading instruction for that letter.
  Say, "We are learning to write letter **a**. Letter **a** makes the /a/ sound."
- During reading, integrate handwriting instruction for that letter.
  Say, "Take out your handwriting book. Go to the letter teaching page for **e**. We are going to do an extra handwriting lesson today to learn letter **e**."

3. Follow the reading teaching order
- During reading, teach in the reading order.
- During handwriting, teach in the reading order.
- Use the handwriting letter teaching page you need. Do the word and sentence pages after all the letters have been taught.

SCOPE AND SEQUENCE OF PRINTING

The Scope and Sequence of Printing defines the content and order of printing instruction. The skills needed for printing develop as early as preschool. Although we do not teach printing formally at the preschool level, we can informally create an environment and encourage activities for developing good habits that students need later. The secret is teaching skills in a way that makes learning natural and fun.

Description

Type of Instruction
Informal/Structured: This is a variety of activities that address the broad range of letter and school readiness skills.
Formal/Structured: Teacher directed activities are presented in a more precise order with specific objectives.

Handwriting Sequence
Pre-Strokes: These are beginning marks that are made randomly or deliberately.
Shapes: Shapes often are introduced before letters and are a foundation for letter formation skills.
Capitals/Numbers: These use simple shapes and strokes. They have the same size, start, and position.
Lowercase Letters: These are tall, small, and descending symbols with more complex strokes, sizes, starts, and positions.

Stages of Learning
Pre-Instruction Readiness: This is attention, behavior, language, and fine motor skills for beginning writing.
Stage 1: Imitating the Teacher: This is watching someone form a letter first, and then writing the letter.
Stage 2: Copying Printed Models: This is looking at a letter and then writing the letter.
Stage 3: Independent Writing: This is writing without watching someone or even seeing a letter.

Physical Approach
Crayon Use: Crayons prepare children for using pencils. Using small crayons encourages proper grip.
Pencil Use: Proper pencil use is necessary for good handwriting. In kindergarten, children transfer their crayon grip to pencils.
Posture: Good sitting posture promotes good handwriting. This is taught in kindergarten.
Paper Placement: When children are writing sentences and paragraphs, they're ready to angle the paper so they can move the writing hand easily across the page.

Printing Skills
Primary Skills
   Memory: Remember and write dictated letters and numbers.
   Orientation: Face letters and numbers in the correct direction.
   Start: Begin each letter or number correctly.
   Sequence: Make the letter strokes in the correct order.
Secondary Skills
   Placement: Place letters and numbers on the baseline.
   Size: Write in a consistent, grade appropriate size.
   Spacing: Place letters in words closely, putting space between words.
   Control: Focus on neatness and proportion.

Functional Writing
Letters/Numbers
Words
Sentences
Paragraphs
Writing in All Subjects

SCOPE AND SEQUENCE OF PRINTING

	PK	K	1	2
Type of Instruction				
Informal/Structured	X			
Formal/Structured		X	X	X
Handwriting Sequence				
Pre-Strokes	X			
Shapes	X			
Capitals/Numbers	X	X	X	X
Lowercase Letters	*See note below	X	X	X
Stages of Learning				
Pre-Instruction Readiness	X	X		
Stage 1: Imitating the Teacher	X	X	X	X
Stage 2: Copying Printed Models		X	X	X
Stage 3: Independent Writing		X	X	X
Physical Approach				
Crayon Use	X			
Pencil Use		X	X	X
Posture		X	X	X
Paper Placement		X	X	X
Printing Skills				
Primary Skills				
Memory	X	X	X	X
Orientation	X	X	X	X
Start	X	X	X	X
Sequence	X	X	X	X
Secondary Skills				
Placement		X	X	X
Size		X	X	X
Spacing		X	X	X
Control		X Emerging	X	X
Functional Writing				
Letters/Numbers	X Capitals/Numbers	X	X	
Words		X Short	X Short	X Long
Sentences		X Short	X Short	X Long
Paragraphs			X Short	X Long
Writing in All Subjects		X	X	X

*Children in preschool are taught lowercase letter recognition–but not writing. They may be taught the lowercase letters in their names.

STAGES OF LEARNING

Now that you understand printing skills and the role you play in developing handwriting, it will help you understand the stages of learning. Children typically learn in a developmental order. Too often, we find ourselves in such a hurry that we rush ahead. Children learn to write correctly and easily when instructions follow these developmentally based stages. You may need to review some of the pre-instructional readiness concepts below before advancing to the more formal instructional steps that follow:

Pre-Instructional Readiness (Pre-K and Kindergarten)

Make Mat Man™
Take turns. Learn body parts and how to draw with Mat Man.

Sing & Imitate
Join the class to sing about shapes, letters, numbers, and even how to say hello!

Build Letters
Know how to pick and place Wood Pieces to build letters.
(D = one big line + one big curve)

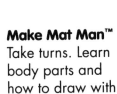

Trace on a Slate
Make capitals and numbers on a reversal-proof slate! Do it with multisensory Wet–Dry–Try.

Share, Play, Socialize
Participate, take turns, and communicate with materials, music, and teacher modeling.

Color and Write
Practice in a child friendly workbook, with pictures and models that promote good habits.

Instructional Stages

When the pre-instructional readiness skills have been established, handwriting instruction proceeds in three stages (Imitation, Copying, and Independent Writing). Multisensory activities can enhance learning in every stage.

Stage 1 – Imitation

The child watches as the teacher writes and then imitates the teacher.

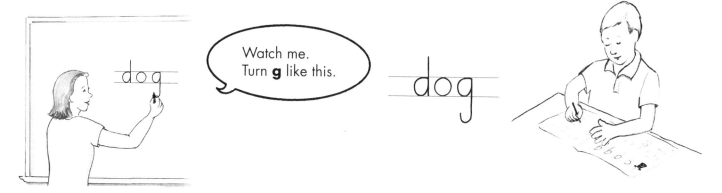

See the motions as the teacher writes step-by-step.

Hear the directions.

See the model.

Write **dog**.

Stage 2 – Copying

The child looks at the completed model of a letter, word, or sentence and copies it, trying to match the model.

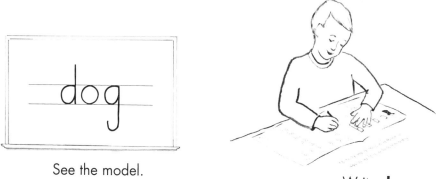

See the model.

Write **dog**.

Stage 3 – Independent Writing

The child writes unassisted, without a demonstration or a model.

Write **dog**.

ABOUT EMERGING WRITERS

When children enter kindergarten, we have no way of knowing their handwriting experience. Regardless of their level of preparedness, you can help them become emergent writers by showing them the way. Learning handwriting is like learning to ride a bike. We start by giving the child a tricycle, then training wheels, and finally two wheels. Unfortunately, in today's world, we find ourselves giving the two wheels before the training. The skill of handwriting will emerge only through proper instruction.

As we discuss the emergent writer, two questions often arise:
1. Is it okay for children to free write?
2. How soon can kindergarteners write in journals?

Here's what we think…

Free Writing - Is it Okay?

Free writing is letting children write without specific instruction. We consider two types of free writing. One is directly tied to what some consider to be handwriting instruction (see Sample 1). The other is tied to children curiously forming letters and numbers from what is referred to as "Environmental Print" (see Sample 2).

Sample 1 - Free writing as the means for learning handwriting is trouble. When teaching handwriting, it isn't appropriate to just pass out worksheets for the children to practice. Children who are left to their own resources to learn how to write letters become self-taught writers. Their completed letters may look okay, but the letters often are formed with inconsistent or bad habits. These children may survive the kindergarten work load, but fall apart when the writing demands increase. These children often need remediation simply because they weren't taught.

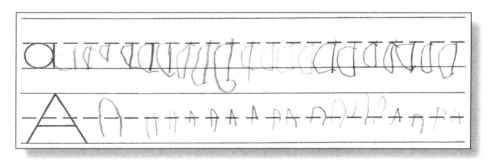

Sample 2 - Environmental printing is just fine but it needs to be followed by explicit instruction of how to write the letters. Once taught, children must stick consistently to the new correct habit. Environmental printing won't lead to any ingrained bad habits as long as you follow up with explicit instruction.

Journal Writing

Journal writing in kindergarten is a common practice. When is it appropriate for kindergarteners to write in journals? The answer depends on the function of the journal and what you are hoping to teach.

To give children the best experience for success, teach them their letters first and then have them transition to journal writing as they develop the ability to combine letters into words and words into sentences. As ideal as that sounds, we also understand there are several reasons beyond handwriting for exposing children to journal writing.

Journal writing in kindergarten is similar to free writing. As long as students get proper handwriting instruction, journal writing at any stage should not be a problem. You might not have the best looking journals in the first few months of school, but if you want to expose students to the process of writing, then it's okay to introduce journal writing.

Tips

1. Have beginning writers draw a picture as an adult models the writing.
2. Choose words from a group of letters the children have learned in handwriting. For example, after they learn **c o s v w a d g**, you can model the words **dog**, **good**, **dad**, etc., for them to write in their journals. They can then draw a picture of their choice.
3. Consider waiting until students have learned all of their lowercase letters. See the example below. This child drew a picture at the start of the school year. The teacher modeled the writing with the sentences the child dictated. By spring, the child was writing beautifully on her own.

By spring, the child was writing independently.

Get Ready for Readiness

Many of your kindergarteners may have been exposed to a variety of readiness skills in preschool. Many have not. Therefore, assume that all children could benefit from a thorough readiness overview. The next section of this guide is dedicated to getting your kindergarteners off to the best start. Some of the information is a review of what we teach at the preschool level. This information is valuable to you because some students in your room may need to review these most basic skills. The other activities and information we provide apply to all of your students and explain why we do things at this particular level. If you are confident that your students are ready for letter instruction, skip to page 74.

The activities on the next several pages may be basic for your kindergarteners, but are a fun way to reinforce important teaching concepts. Skim through the next several pages to see if there is something you would like to mix into your lessons and to understand how HWT prepares younger children for success.

EASEL ART AND FINE MOTOR

An Easel to Share

Standing up and working against gravity helps build strength in the shoulders and arms. An easel is ideal for wrist position too. You may want to consider turning an old bi-fold door into a big community easel. In preschool and even in kindergarten, we suggest putting less experienced children by the more experienced. Children learn through imitation. Because it's a communal picture, there is no concern about the final product. It's as appealing as graffiti. Place small baskets of FLIP Crayons™ around the easel. Let children doodle freely.

Fine Motor Skills

Many of the preschool activities incorporate fine motor experiences. Often, kindergarteners (especially boys) need some additional fine motor support. Consider using the *Get Set For School Sing Along* CD, Tracks 10 and 16, for finger play activities. For more tips for fine motor practice and ideas you can send home to parents, visit, **www.hwtears.com/click**.

FUN REVIEW WITH PRE-K MUSIC

Music is a big part of our readiness curriculum. You can use the award winning *Get Set for School Sing Along* CD to review positional concepts, body parts, and letter formation. You can also use some of these songs to vary some of the multisensory learning activities that are part of the kindergarten curriculum. It's easy—the lyrics tell students what to do. You can find the lyrics to each song in the booklet enclosed with the CD.

Songs for Readiness

Track #	Song	Suggested Activities
1	**Where Do You Start Your Letters?**	Reach to the TOP!
2	**Alphabet Song**	Point and sing with Print Wall Cards
3	**Alphabet Song (Instrumental)**	Point and sing with Print Wall Cards
4	**There's a Dog in the School**	Bark to the alphabet
5	**Crayon Song**	Learn to hold crayons correctly
6	**Magic C**	Finger trace Magic Cs in the air
7	**Hello Song**	Practice social skills, right/left orientation
8	**Mat Man**	Sing, build, and draw Mat Man™
9	**Count on Me**	Count 1 and 2 using body parts
10	**Five Fingers Play**	Do a fun fingerplay to teach the concept of 5
11	**Toe Song**	Wiggle your toes and learn about 10
12	**Bird Legs**	Count bird legs and learn about 2
13	**Animal Legs**	Count animal legs and learn about 4
14	**The Ant, the Bug & the Bee**	Learn about 6 and up, down, and all around
15	**Spiders Love to Party**	Dance like spiders and learn about 8
16	**Ten Little Fingers**	Do a fingerplay that teaches 10
17	**My Teacher Draws**	Sing as the teacher draws a shape
18	**Puffy Fluffy**	Explore the vertical down stroke with movement
19	**Tap, Tap, Tap**	Explore positional concepts with Wood Pieces
20	**Golden Slippers**	Explore with Wood Pieces
21	**Skip to My Lou**	Practice gross motor movement to a familiar tune
22	**Down on Grandpa's Farm**	Sing about farm animals
23	**Peanut Butter and Jelly**	Learn sequencing and following directions
24	**Rain Song**	Sing and color
25	**Wood Piece Pokey**	Have *Hokey Pokey* fun using Wood Pieces

SHAKE HANDS WITH ME

This activity teaches right/left discrimination and an important social skill: greeting others.

Preparation
Each day, choose a different sensory stimulus (touch, scent, liquid, solid, visual, auditory).
Here are a few suggestions:
- Lotion, rubber stamp, flavoring, water in a bowl, and so forth

Directions
1. Shake hands with each child. Smile, make eye contact, and say, "Hello."
2. Say, "This is your right hand. I'm going to do something to your right hand."
   Lotion—Put a dab on the right thumb and index finger. "Rub your fingers together."
   Rubber Stamp—Stamp the right hand. "Look at your right hand now."
   Flavoring—Dab some flavoring (e.g. peppermint) on the right index finger. "Smell that peppermint."
3. Direct students to raise their right hands and say with you:
   - "This is my right hand."
   - "I shake hands with my right hand."

Skills Developed
- Social Skills—For meeting and greeting
- Right/Left Discrimination—Only the right hand is for shaking
- Directionality—A sense of directionality with the body

Tips
- Encourage children to greet others and practice shaking hands with one another.
- When you raise your right hand with your students, make sure you are facing the same direction they are.

LEARNING THE TOP!

English is a top-to-bottom, left-to-right language. That's the way we read and write. The top-to-bottom habit is the key to printing quickly and neatly. Children who start letters at the top don't have to think about making letters. They can print automatically and quickly without becoming sloppy. Starting at the bottom causes difficulty because it is impossible to write quickly without becoming sloppy. This demonstration proves the importance of starting at the top. Try it!

Make 5 lines down.　　Make 5 lines, alternating down/up.　　　　Now do it again, quickly.

↓ slow | | | | |　　　　↓↑ slow | | | | |　　　　↓ fast | | | | |　　↓↑ fast (| \ | |

By starting at the top, you can be both fast and neat. Children who start letters at the bottom often are slow or sloppy.

Sing About It – *Where Do You Start Your Letters?*

In this guide, you'll learn how to correct bad habits and emphasize good ones with easy and fun techniques. Start by teaching this fun song. You know the tune: *If You're Happy and You Know It.* The lyrics for *Where Do You Start Your Letters?* are below. Be sure to also try our rock-n-roll version (it includes numbers too). You can find it on our *Rock, Rap, Tap & Learn* CD, Track 2. A slower version is available on our *Get Set for School Sing Along* CD, Track 1. Children will have great fun singing and dancing while learning the difference between top, bottom, and middle.

Chords
F = C F A
C7 = C E G B♭
B♭ = F B♭ D

Where Do You Start Your Letters?

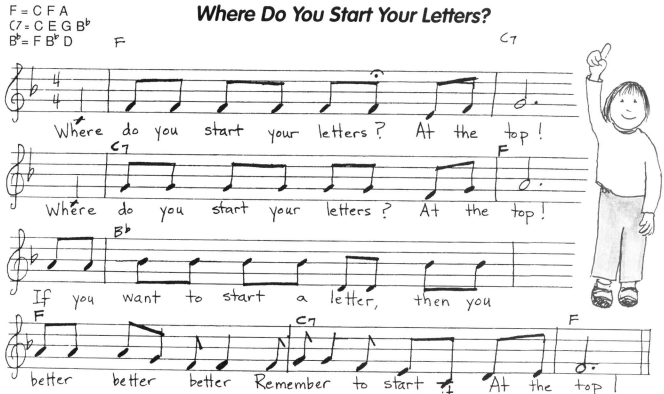

Where do you start your letters? At the top!
Where do you start your letters? At the top!
If you want to start a letter, then you
better better better Remember to start it At the top!

Use this song when you're teaching or reviewing PRINTED CAPITALS.

Tune: *If You're Happy and You Know It*

BASIC STROKES: SIGN IN PLEASE!

Because some letters are easier to form than others, in pre-k and kindergarten we teach pre-strokes to children based on developmental principles.*

Studies show that children gradually develop the ability to copy forms in a very predictable order as shown below:

* Gessell, Arnold, and others. The First Years of Life. New York: Harper and Row. 1940.

Alphabet Sign-In

This activity is fun and develops many important skills. Kindergarteners can have fun by signing in alphabetically.

Preparation

1. Prepare blackboard with a wide stop line near the bottom. (A blackboard is best, but you can use a white board.)
2. Break chalk into small ½" pieces to encourage correct grip.

Directions

1. Teacher prints **A**.
   - Write **A** up high, but within children's reach.
   - Teach **A** and each letter that follows as you write.
   - Use consistent words as you demonstrate: **A** = big line, big line, and little line.
2. Teacher asks, "Whose name begins with **A**? Adam!"
3. Adam comes to the board and you introduce him, saying: "This is…" (children say "Adam").
   "Adam starts with…" (children say **A**).
   "In Adam's name, the **A** makes the sound…" (children make the **A** sound).
4. Adam signs in by making a big line down from **A**. He stops on the line.
5. Repeat this exercise with each letter. Children sign in alphabetically.

Skills Developed

- Top-to-bottom letter formation
- Stopping on a line
- Names of capital letters and of classmates
- Letter sounds using classmates' names
- Big line, little line, big curve, little curve to understand the parts of each capital letter
- Alphabetical order
- Left-to-right sequencing
- Social skills including following directions, cooperating, listening, taking turns, interacting in groups
- Chalk and pencil grip
- Number concepts including counting and comparing by counting the lines for each letter.

Variation

You can change how children sign in to teach other skills:

- Horizontal line skills: underline letter from left to right
- Circle skills: circle the letter by starting at the top with a **C** stroke

CRAYON GRIP

Little Hands, Little Crayons

With all the fun writing tools available today it's hard to decide which are age appropriate. The crayon is the best tool for preparing a child for handwriting. Crayons create a natural resistance and build strength in the hand. Our FLIP Crayons™ are perfect for little hands because they require children to hold the crayons with their fingertips. In addition, the dual colors and tips encourage children to flip the crayons while coloring, promoting the development of fine motor skills. FLIP Crayons™ are great for kindergarteners, who will be excited to color with something unique. When students are ready for formal handwriting instruction, introduce a pencil.

Teaching Crayon Grip

You can use strategies from our preschool program to help you further develop grip in kindergarten. If we teach children how to hold their crayons correctly, that skill will progress to proper pencil grip. If you need more activities to promote good crayon and pencil grips try these:

1. Use *Crayon Song* from the *Get Set For School Sing Along* CD, Track 5.
2. Aim and Scribble activities encourage good grip. See the *Pre-K Teacher's Guide* for more information.
3. Don't forget to demonstrate, demonstrate, demonstrate.

COLORING

Coloring is such a common activity that we forget the great benefits it has for developing coordination, grip, and strength. By observing how a child colors, you can determine handwriting readiness. Observe the following skills:

- Attention
- Crayon grip
- Control
- Posture, strength, endurance
- Use of the helping hand

Most kindergarteners still need help with coloring. To help them color:

1. Choose easy to color, appealing pictures.
2. Help them hold the crayon.
3. Demonstrate coloring on a separate page.
   - Side to side (horizontal) strokes
   - Up and down strokes
   - Little circular motions
   - Staying in the lines or following the direction of the lines
4. Encourage children to draw on their pictures.

Typically, the shape of the picture will determine the stroke a child chooses. See the crayon stroke pattern on the cow. If students can't organize their strokes to accommodate the shape of the picture, encourage them to color up/down because that is easiest.

CAPITALIZING ON THE CAPITALS

Teachers agree that capitals are easier, and that's where we begin. When children learn to write their capitals, they develop a strong foundation for printing. They learn important handwriting rules (such as a top-to-bottom, left-to-right habit), proper letter formation, and solid visual memory for capital letters.

Children who learn capitals first, also learn the following:
- Start letters at the top.
- Use the correct stroke sequence to form letters.
- Orient letters and numbers correctly—no reversals!

Learning capitals first makes learning lowercase letters a breeze. Think about it: **c o s v w x y z** are the same as capitals; **j k t p** and **u** also are similar to their capital partners. If we teach capitals correctly, we have already prepared children for nearly half of the lowercase alphabet.

Why Are Capitals Easier Than Lowercase Letters?

Capital letters are easy
- All start at the top.
- All are the same height.
- All occupy the same vertical space.
- All are easy to recognize and identify (compare **A B D G P Q** with **a b d g p q**).
- Capitals are big, bold, and familiar.

Lowercase letters are more difficult
- Lowercase letters start in four different places (**a b e f**).
- Lowercase letters are not the same size. Fourteen letters are half the size of capitals. Twelve are the same size as capitals.
- Lowercase letters occupy three different vertical positions – small, tall, descending.
- Lowercase letters are more difficult to recognize because of subtle differences (**a b d g p q**).

Let's do the math
You can see at a glance that capitals are easier for children. Students have fewer chances to make mistakes when they write capital letters. They aim the pencil at the top and get it right. With lowercase, there are many more variables.

When teaching handwriting, teach capitals first. You will save yourself time, make life easier for children, and get better handwriting results.

CAPITAL AND LOWERCASE LETTER ANALYSIS		
	Capitals	**Lowercase**
Start	1	4
Size	1	2
Position	1	3
Appearance	• Familiar • Distinctive A B D G P Q	• Many similar • Easy to confuse a b d g p q

A PRE-PENCIL, PRE-PAPER START

Children who use HWT in preschool and kindergarten benefit from unique pre-pencil and paper lessons for learning capital letters. In preschool and kindergarten, children use the Wood Pieces Set for Capital Letters to learn letter formation. We give these pieces unique names to teach capitals with consistency.

Children make letters with the Capital Letter Cards, Mat, and Slate. All have a smiley face in the top left corner. These tools help students form each letter correctly, systematically, and without reversals.

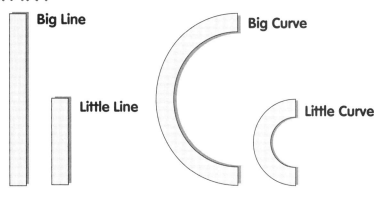

Big Line

Little Line

Big Curve

Little Curve

The Secret of the Smile

The smiley face shows that the letter is right side up and promotes the top-to-bottom, left-to-right habits.

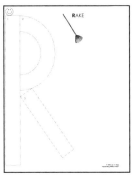

Capital Letter Card

Mat

Slate

Teach kindergarteners capital letter language (big line, little line, big curve, little curve) by modeling letters. Say each stroke as you demonstrate the letter. Even children who are unfamiliar with HWT concepts will learn the names quickly. The Slate is a perfect way for all your students to review their capitals. You only need to teach pre-k readiness activities if students can't remember how to form more than 50 percent of their capital letters.

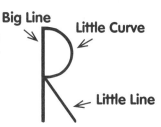

Big Line

Little Curve

Little Line

Fun Review with Pre-K Music

Music is a big part of our readiness curriculum. The *Get Set for School Sing Along* CD is packed with great songs that review ABCs, positional concepts, body parts, and letter formation. It's easy—the lyrics tell students what to do. You can find the song lyrics in the booklet enclosed with the CD. The full listing of songs is on page 17.

The Pre-K Workbook

Get Set for School helps young children learn pre-strokes, shapes, letters, and numbers by tracing a gray crayon stroke. Crayon strokes are seen as complete strokes. Each symbol is indicated with an ⇩ or ☺ icon so children know where to place the crayon.

Children also learn coloring, counting, language skills, writing capitals, and lowercase letter recognition.

NOTE: Kindergarten teachers might want to have a few preschool workbooks on hand for children who need extra practice with strokes, shapes, coloring, grip, etc.

LETTER PLAY

Letter Play is a large piece of our multisensory experiences at the preschool level. Many kindergarten teachers tell us that they implement these two activities successfully during center-based learning.

Roll Letters with Me!

Help children form capital letters out of dough. This activity helps children build strength in their fingers and hands while learning capital letter recognition.

Preparation

1. Roll-A-Dough Tray
2. Dough
3. Roll-A-Dough Tray Cards

Directions

1. Teacher shows how to roll dough (like making a rope or a snake).
2. Children imitate.
3. Teacher shows how to cut and place dough pieces to form a letter. (Use the tray card or just the tray.)
4. Children imitate.

Tips for Teachers

- To see the stroke formation sequence, see page 166.
- Use the Roll-A-Dough tray for more sensory experiences with letters. Put shaving cream, sand, pudding, or finger paint in the tray. Then have the child "write" the capital letter with a finger.

Making Letters on the Stamp and See Screen™

Children learn how to make the capital letters step-by-step. The teacher shows how to stamp the pieces in the correct position and sequence. Later children may use the magnetic chalk to write the letter on the screen.

Preparation

1. Stamp and See Screen™
2. Magnetic big line, little line, big curve, little curve

Directions

1. Teacher stamps the first piece on the screen and then erases it.
2. Children imitate.
3. Teacher stamps the complete letter, step-by-step and then erases it.
4. Children imitate.
5. Children use the magnetic chalk to trace the letter and then they erase it.
6. Children make letter from memory using the pieces or the magnetic chalk.

Tips for Teachers

- Don't erase the screen too quickly. Allow ample time for the student to study the screen.
- Play Mystery Letter game (See page 56 of this guide). First person stamps a big line on the left edge of screen. The other person makes a mystery letter by stamping pieces on the right side. The first person doesn't know what the letter will be.
- Use the Roll-A-Dough Tray Cards. Choose a card, place it on the magnetic screen, have your student trace over the letter with the magnetic chalk. Remove the card to see the letter on the screen. Retrace now.

TRACING SECRETS

Tracing letters has always been popular. Unlike standard dotted tracing, we recommend tracing on a gray crayon stroke. A solid line gives children a sense of letter completeness. The color gray is a good option because it disappears when a child traces over it. Tracing is good only when it is accompanied by adult demonstration.

If you want to do some tracing with kindergarten students:

• Use a highlighter pen or gray crayon to make letters.

• Stay away from dots! Dots are visually confusing and some children will even take the time to connect one dot to the next.

• Clearly indicate (see arrow on the right above A) where the child should start the stroke. We use this special icon in our *Get Set for School* workbook. When making your own tracing activities, a tiny star or small dot will do.

• Provide tracing tips and activities for children to use at home. Often, children get their first experiences with tracing from their parents.

A Tracing Activity - HWT Capital and Number Practice Strips

When teaching children their names, phone numbers, and simple words, consider using a gray crayon and our Capital and Number Practice Strips. Phone numbers are a great place to start.

Preparation
1. Gather one Capital and Number Practice Strip.
2. Have a gray crayon and other colored crayons available.

Directions
1. Adult uses the gray crayon to model one number at a time.
2. Child chooses a different color to trace the adult's model.

Skills Developed
• Letter/number recognition
• Letter/number formation
• Life skills (name, phone number)
• Word recognition

Tips
• Have children practice saying the numbers out loud.
• Go on a hunt for words written with only capitals. Bring the list back to class and write the words on the strips for children to trace.

HELP ME WRITE MY NAME

Children love their names! Do your students recognize their names? Do you see them trying to write their names? How exciting! Teaching a child to write his or her name depends on two things:

1. Age
2. Readiness

To teach developmentally, we suggest teaching name in capitals in preschool and transition to name in title case at the end of preschool or the start of kindergarten when children are ready.

Start of Preschool and Start of Kindergarten — NAME

When you think it's time to help a child write letters, start with capitals. Capitals are the easiest to write and recognize. They are all the same height and all start at the same place (the TOP).

Students won't always write in capitals, but it's the easiest way for them to start. You can explain that there are two ways to write a name. The big letter way and the small letter way. Show them both, and then tell them the secret: their hands are growing and they are ready to learn the big letter way. When they get big and their hands get stronger, they can learn the other way too. Children will follow your lead.

We suggest:

1. Displaying names both ways in the room: all caps and title case
2. Teaching name in all caps through careful demonstration and imitation activities

To Teach NAME in Preschool

1. Use the Capital and Number Practice strips.
2. Put your strip above the child's strip. Demonstrate each letter on your strip and wait for the child to imitate you. Do this letter by letter (see below).

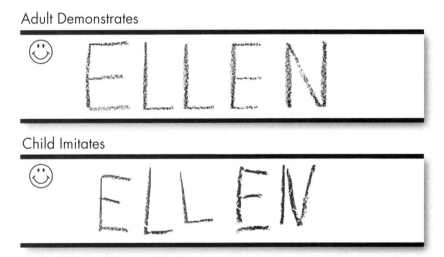

End of Preschool and Start of Kindergarten: Name

You may choose to stay with name in all caps for a short time until you feel students have had enough practice with their lowercase letters. Most children look forward to learning new skills. Now is a perfect time to transition them from writing their names in all caps to title case. With the experience of being able to write their names correctly in all capitals, they will then transition to title case correctly and easily. For tips on teaching names in title case using Wet–Dry–Try, turn to page 49 of this guide. For additional activities to teach names in title case, visit **www.hwtears.com/click**.

Educate Parents

Teaching children their names is a great activity to send home with parents.
Visit **www.hwtears.com/click** to print activities for teaching names in capitals and in title case.

Help Me Write My Name

"That's my name. My name starts with _____." Maybe your child is trying to write or even make letters you can recognize. If so, then it's time to start demonstrating how to write a few letters. Here's how:

1. Be a good example.
2. Write in all capitals.
3. Start every letter at the top.
4. Teach letters step-by-step.
5. Write on paper strips with a smiley face in the top left corner.

For Parents

How can I be a good example?
Hold the crayon correctly. Your child will be watching how you make the letters and how you hold the crayon or pencil. Be a good model. You may need to make a special effort to hold the crayon correctly.

Why should I use all capitals?
Capitals are the first letters that children can recognize and remember visually. They are the first letters children can write physically. If a child can write his or her name correctly in capitals, you may introduce lowercase letters.

Does it matter where my student starts?
Yes, it does. English has one basic rule for both reading and writing: read and write from top to bottom, left to right. When you write with a child, always start at the top.

What do I say when I teach the letters?
Always say, "I start at the top." Then describe the part you're making. Say "big" or "little" for size. Say "line" or "curve" for shape, like this: **D** = "I start at the top. I make a big line. Now I make a big curve."

What do I use and how do I do this?
Use two strips of paper: one for you and one for the child. Place your strip directly above the child's and demonstrate the first letter in the child's name. Say each step as you make the letter. Be sure the child can see the strokes as you write. (Avoid blocking the child's view with your hand.) Then tell the child to make the letter on his/her paper. Say the steps as the child writes, encouraging the child to say the steps aloud with you. Continue letter by letter.

NOTE:
To make paper strips – Use a standard sheet. Fold it in half the long way, and then in half again. Cut on folds to make 4 strips.

Extra help – If the child has difficulty imitating your letter, you may use a gray crayon to pre-write each letter on the child's paper. Do this letter by letter and let the child crayon trace over your letter. Make your gray letters progressively lighter and discontinue pre-writing as child gains ability.

HANDWRITING INSTRUCTION
Choose Your Approach

The right approach to handwriting instruction is the one that is best for you and your students. Teachers, like students, approach handwriting with different skills.

New to Handwriting Instruction?
Most teachers were never taught to teach handwriting. In fact, one survey reports that 90 percent of teachers surveyed say they don't feel appropriately trained to teach handwriting. Regardless of your experience, you can be successful this year with a steady, consistent approach.

Veteran Teacher of Handwriting?
Some teachers have strong skills for teaching and assessing their students' handwriting needs. They have developed an approach that works and can easily adapt to meet individual and class differences. These teachers like to try new things and are good problem solvers. If this describes you, then you should take a flexible, varied approach to handwriting.

STEADY INSTRUCTION
You—new to handwriting, a little unsure
Your students—some with strong skills; others with weak skills and poor habits
How to Do It
1. Read this guide carefully.
   - Use the Posture, Paper, and Pencil activities on page 60-65.
2. Use all the suggested multisensory lessons to support your teaching.
3. Follow the *Letters and Numbers for Me* workbook page by page.
   - Teach capital letters.
   - Follow a pace that suits your class for lowercase, word, sentences, and activity pages.

FLEXIBLE INSTRUCTION
You—trained and experienced
Your students—some with strong skills; others with weak skills and poor habits
How to Do It
1. Scan this guide, looking for new ideas or information.
   - Use the Posture, Paper, and Pencil strategies and Pencil activities on page 60-65.
2. Choose selected multisensory lessons to support your teaching.
3. Follow a flexible approach to *Letters and Numbers for Me*.
   - Teach capital letters.
   - Teach lowercase letters.

Kindergarten Instruction Overview: Don't skip Pencil Pick-Ups...all children need practice holding their pencils correctly. See page 78 of this guide.

Multisensory Lessons

Goodbye to boring handwriting drills. Hello to fun and achievement! Research supports the importance of multisensory teaching to address children's diverse learning styles: visual, tactile, auditory, and kinesthetic. We encourage you to include the multisensory activities in the classroom to appeal to different learning styles and make lessons more fun.

The Handwriting Without Tears® program goes beyond typical multisensory instruction. Our strategies and materials are exceptional and uniquely effective at facilitating dynamic classrooms. Here are just a few teaching methods:

Visual
- Step-by-step illustrations of letter formation give clear visual direction.
- Clean, uncluttered black and white pages are presented in a visually simple format.
- Illustrations in workbooks face left to right, promoting left-to-right directionality.

Tactile
- Wet–Dry–Try on a slate or blackboard gives children touch and repetition without boredom.
- Step-by-step workbook models are big enough for finger tracing.
- The frame of the Slate helps children make lines and keep letters and numbers well proportioned.

Auditory
- Consistent, child-friendly language helps children learn and remember easily.
- Music and different voices promote memorable and entertaining letter instruction.
- Unique Mystery Letters prevent children from using old bad habits by delaying the auditory letter cue.

Kinesthetic
- Music and movement teach letter formation.
- Door Tracing and Imaginary Writing teach using large arm movements and visual cues.

We assigned an interactive activity to each letter lesson. Don't be limited by our suggestions. You can use most of the activities with all letters.

Below is the list of our multisensory lessons that are described on the following pages.
- Music and Movement
- Wood Pieces
- Mat Man™
- Wet–Dry–Try
- Door Tracing
- Imaginary Writing
- Letter Size and Place
- Voices
- Mystery Letters
- Letter Stories
- Magic C* and Diver Letters School*

*These lessons are specific to a group of letters and are included with the letter lessons for each group.

Tips
- Prepare ahead
- Be dynamic and silly
- Sing
- Encourage your students to participate
- Share techniques with parents
- Create your own activities

MUSIC AND MOVEMENT

The *Rock, Rap, Tap & Learn* CD is loaded with upbeat songs to make handwriting fun. The best thing about music is that it promotes movement. Whether you are teaching descending letters or spacing skills, this CD has all you need to charge up your lessons and catch your students' attention. The lyrics are on the jacket cover of the CD. The following is a list of suggested activities for each song.

Track #	Song	Suggested Activities
1	**Alphabet Boogie**	This song will have your students doing a simple boogie to the ABCs. It is a great warm-up because it reviews the letters and sounds of the alphabet.
2	**Where Do You Start Your Letters**?	Play a question and answer game with students. Move to the song: reach to the top, bottom, and shake it in the middle. Share the song with parents.
3	**Air Writing**	Choose a letter and trace it in the air for your class. Have students follow along and trace with you. See page 52.
4	**Hey, Hey! Big Line**	Use Wood Pieces to review positional concepts. All you need are the big lines.
5	**Diagonals**	Children learn the diagonal stroke with ease by taking an arm, reaching for the top, and sliding down at an angle.
6	**Big Line March**	Children will have a great time marching around with big lines. They can move, tap, and dance to this song for positional concept review.
7	**Sentence Song**	Model a sentence (no more than three words) on the board. Point to the capital, the words, and the spaces, and ending punctuation as the children sing. You can also have children write a sentence and point to the sentence parts as they sing.
8	**My Bonnie Lies over the Ocean**	Have your students sit or stand every time they hear a word starting with **b**. They need to listen more carefully as the song gets faster.
9	**Picking Up My Pencil**	Students learn proper pencil grip with this entertaining exercise. See page 63 for more tips on grips.
10	**Stomp Your Feet**	Students learn proper pencil grip and posture with this entertaining exercise. See page 61 for more about posture.
11	**Vowels**	This song helps students review the vowels and teaches the difference between capital and lowercase sizes.

Track #	Song	Suggested Activities
12	**Frog Jump Letters**	Children stand up and finger trace the Frog Jump Capitals in the air. Let children jump around between letter exercises. The Frog Jump Capitals are **F E D P B R N M**.
13	**Give It a Middle**	This song helps children learn the middle of **A G** and **H**. Children finger trace or watch as you model letters **A G** and **H** on the board while the song plays.
14	**Give It a Top**	Children learn about letters **T J I**. They follow you as you model these letters on the board or in the air.
15	**Sliding Down to the End of the Alphabet**	Start with **V** and slide all the way down to **Z**. This rock-n-roll song will never let children forget the ending of the alphabet. It's also great diagonal practice.
16	**CAPITALS & lowercase**	Teach letters **Cc Oo Ss Vv Ww** (easy capital/lowercase partners). Emphasize capital and lowercase sizes.
17	**Magic C Rap**	Children learn how to use **c** to make **a d g o q** with this memorable rap. See page 117 for more.
18	**Diver Letters' School**	This song incorporates movement to teach the Diver Letter group **p r n m h b**. See page 128 for more.
19	**Descending Letters**	Children will always remember lowercase **g j y p q**. Model these letters on the board. Point out that **g** and **j** go down and turn, **y** goes sliding down, **p** goes straight down, **q** goes down and makes a u-turn.
20	**Number Song**	Write numbers on paper or in the air as you use this song to review number formation.
21	**My Teacher Writes**	Use big line, little line and big curve, little curve to teach your students numbers with this interactive song.
22	**10 Fingers**	Count by tens. Five children line up side-by-side. As the chant plays children step forward and hold up their 10 fingers. Don't just stop at 50!
23	**Mat Man Rock**	Use this song to review body parts, encourage group activity and participation, building, and counting.
24	**Head & Shoulders, Baby!**	This is a great song for warming up bodies or reviewing body parts. Children who participate will work out their wiggles and be ready to learn.
25	**Tapping to the ABCs**	The name says it all. Children can tap on their desks as they review their ABCs.

WOOD PIECES SET

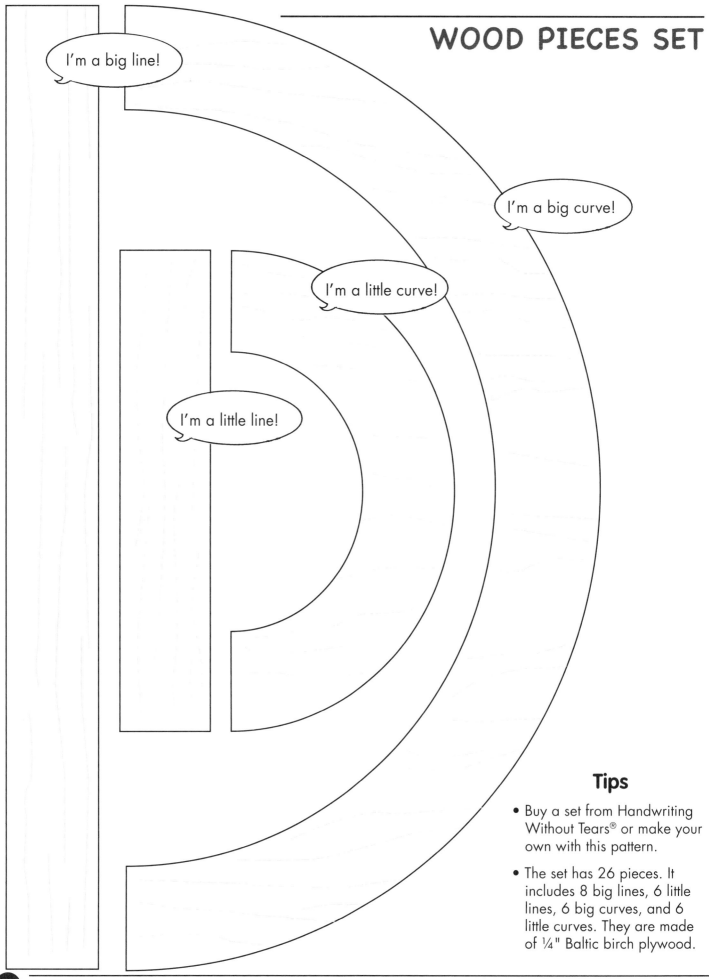

I'm a big line!

I'm a big curve!

I'm a little curve!

I'm a little line!

Tips

- Buy a set from Handwriting Without Tears® or make your own with this pattern.

- The set has 26 pieces. It includes 8 big lines, 6 little lines, 6 big curves, and 6 little curves. They are made of ¼" Baltic birch plywood.

Preparing for Wood Pieces

There are several ways the Wood Pieces can be used. Many people besides teachers use the Wood Pieces: parents, tutors, homeschoolers, and therapists. That's because they are highly versatile and can be used in many ways; in many places.

We have some advice for you so when you use the Wood Pieces, you and your students will get the most out of the experience.

One-on-One
Number of Wood Piece sets: 1

If seated:
Child sits beside the adult

Small Group
Number of Wood Piece sets: 1 set per 4 children

If seated:
• Children sit in front of the teacher or in a small group on the floor

As a Class
Number of Wood Piece sets: 1 set per 4 children

If seated:
• At their tables or desks with teacher in the front of room
  In a circle on the floor with teacher in the middle

NOTE: If listening to *Rock, Rap, Tap & Learn* CD: Students move their bodies around the room and move the wood pieces along to the song.

Introducing Wood Pieces

Working with Wood Pieces is a fun and relaxed way to teach children the concepts and words to describe size and shape. This activity prepares children for making capital letters.

Preparation
1. Set Wood Pieces in front of children.
2. Use *Hey, Hey Big Line,* Track 4, and *Big Line March,* Track 6, from the *Rock, Rap, Tap & Learn* CD.

*Additional Activities:
Get Set For School Sing Along CD
Tracks 19, 20, 25

Directions
1. Introduce children to the names of the Wood Pieces.
   We are very particular about their names.
      "This is a big line." (Holding it up in the air.)
      "Can you show me a big line?" (Children hold it up in the air.)
2. Repeat for other shapes.
      "This is a little line. Can you show me a little line?"
      "This is a big curve. Can you show me a big curve?"
      "This is a little curve. Can you show me a little curve?"
3. Play songs from the CD and have children participate while the music plays.

Skills Developed
1. Language skills
2. Size and shape concepts

Tips
1. You can introduce Wood Pieces to an entire class or to small groups during centers.
2. Don't stop with the activities we suggest. You can create some of your own.

Why Wood Pieces?
How do you teach capital letter **R**? Which verbal directions do you use? If you asked 10 teachers that same question, you would be amazed at the response. Ten different teachers, 10 different responses. Thus, the reason for Wood Pieces. With Wood Pieces, we all say the same thing. You can't beat that type of consistency!

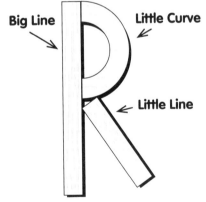

Children learn through consistency. The Wood Pieces allow children to build their capital letters (with exception of **J** and **U**) using 4 basic shapes. By using the Wood Pieces, we can build strong foundation skills for letter memory, orientation, and sequencing.

Beyond learning letters, we also use Wood Pieces to teach children the following:
- Socialization
- Body Awareness
- Prepositions
- Taking Turns
- Motor Movements
- Following Directions
- Stroke Exploration
- Patterns
- Counting

Polish, Stack, Sort, and Trade Wood Pieces

Children love to feel like they are part of a group. Spread the Wood Pieces on the floor and have children sit around them.

Preparation
1. Scatter Wood Pieces on the floor
2. Gather cloth pieces for polishing

Directions
1. Show children how to polish, stack, and sort the Wood Pieces. This is a friendly, relaxed, and worthwhile activity that they love.
2. Talk about the pieces. Gradually, children will pick up the important words (big line, little line, big curve, little curve) along with the pieces. You can say:

> "You have a big curve. I have a big curve. We picked the same pieces."
> "You have a big line. I have a big curve. Do you want to trade?"
> "Let's polish lines. Do you want to polish a big line or a little line?"
> "It's time to collect the Wood Pieces. Who has a big line?"

Skills Developed
- Size and Shape—Children can feel and see the difference between big and little, line and curve.
- Vocabulary—Children use consistent words (big line, little line, big curve, little curve) to name the pieces.
- Social Skills—Children learn to work together, share, trade, pay attention, and imitate.
- Bilateral Hand Skills—Using one hand to hold a piece while the other rubs helps develop a child's fine motor skills. Usually children rub with the dominant hand.
- Visual Skills—Children begin to see the differences in sizes and shapes.
- Figure/Ground Discrimination—Students can find a particular piece in an assortment of scattered pieces.

Tips
1. Use socks on hands to rub the Wood Pieces.
2. Make up songs while rubbing. This one goes to *Row, Row, Row Your Boat*:

Rub, rub, rub big line	Rub, rub, rub big curve
Rub your big line	It is nice and round
Rub, rub, rub big line	Rub, rub, rub big curve
It looks just like mine	Now put it on the ground

Wood Pieces in the Bag
Children learn with a sense of touch.

Preparation
Fill a bag with assorted Capital Letter Wood Pieces.

Directions
1. Child reaches inside, feels one piece, guesses which piece it is, and then takes it out.
2. Teacher names a piece for the child to find.

Skills Developed
- Tactile Discrimination of Size and Shape—Children feel the characteristics of the piece they are touching.
- Vocabulary—Children use consistent words to describe size and shape (big line, little line, big curve, and little curve).
- Fine Motor Skills—Children reach in the bag and manipulate the piece with one hand.
- Taking Turns—Children learn to cooperate as they take turns reaching into the bag.
- Socialization—Children speak to their neighbors who are holding the bag for them.

Tip
- You can easily alter the level of this activity just by changing what you put in the bag. For very young children or those with special needs, put in just two different shapes.
- Make it extra fun by adding objects too, like a ping-pong ball or a spoon. Children will use words that describe the size and shape of these objects.
- Sit in a circle as a class and take turns passing around the bag. Children close their eyes and have to find what their classmate suggests.

Positions in Space and Body Parts with Wood Pieces

Children learn word positions and placement skills with Wood Pieces.

Preparation
Each child needs a big line or little line.

Directions
Say the name of each position or body part as you demonstrate. Have children say it too.

UP in the air
Move it UP and DOWN

UNDER your chair
UNDER your arm (one arm out)
OVER your arm

Out to the SIDE
Move it AROUND in circles

Hold it in FRONT of you
Hold it at the BOTTOM
It's VERTICAL

Climb UP and DOWN
Hold it at the BOTTOM, MIDDLE, TOP

Say HORIZONTAL
Move it SIDE to SIDE

Skills Developed
- Imitating—Children learn to watch and follow the teacher.
- Positioning—Children learn to hold and move the pieces in various positions. They learn the words that describe position.

Tips
- Teach other position words such as: BEHIND my back, BETWEEN my fingers, BESIDE me, THROUGH my arm (put hand on hip first), ON my lap.
- When teaching TOP, BOTTOM, MIDDLE use a big line. Teacher holds the big line with just one hand at the BOTTOM, then changes hands and positions, naming the position each time. Children imitate.
- Teach body parts by naming each body part as you touch it with a Wood Piece.

More Positions - Vertical, Horizontal, and Diagonal

By imitating you, children® learn position and placement skills and words.

Preparation
Give each child the pieces to be used.

Directions
Say the name of each position as you demonstrate. Have children say it too.

Hold two big lines in one hand.

Open them! Hold them out. Say, "Voila! It's a **V**." (Guide child in finger tracing the **V**.)

Hold two big lines end to end diagonally. Move and say, "Diagonal, diagonal."

Make a big line stand up. Make it "walk" on your arm.

Now it's tired. Make it lie down.

One big line is standing up. One little line across the top. It's a **T**.

Hold one big line in each hand.

Put them together at the top. Looks like a teepee or the start of the **A**.

Together at the middle—It's an **X**! **X** marks the spot!

Skills Developed
* Vertical and Horizontal—Moving the pieces in vertical and horizontal positions prepares children to make capitals **E F H I L T**.
* Diagonal—Moving the lines diagonally prepares children to make capitals **A K M N R V W X Y Z**. They make **V** and **X** and the beginning of **A**.

Tip
* Encourage children to speak with you. The words vertical, horizontal, and diagonal are fun to say with the motions.

Curves and Circles

By imitating you, children learn to associate shapes with movement.

Preparation
Give each child big or little curves.

Directions
Say the name of each position as you demonstrate. Have children say it too.

APART
Hold the big curves apart.

TOGETHER
Bring them together.

Say "O" or "Zeeeero"
Hold them up to your face.
Make circles in the air now.

RAINBOW—hold a big curve up.
Sing *Somewhere Over the Rainbow*.
Hold the big curve with one hand and
then with the other hand, make big
curve motions in the air.

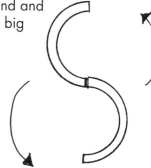

SMILE
Hold big curve up to face.
Make smiles in the air.

SQUIGGLE—WIGGLE
Hold curves with just one end touching.
Move them alternately up or down.

Skills Developed
- Capitals with Curves—Moving and placing the curves prepares children to write the capitals with curves:
  B C D G J O P Q R S.
- Circle—Children learn that this symbol **O** can be a shape (circle), a letter (**O**) and a number (**0**).
- Associate Movement with Shape—Moving the arm in an arc or circle prepares children for writing curves and circles.

Capitals with Letter Cards

Teach children how to place Wood Pieces on the Letter Cards. Do one to three capitals each session. Use this lesson plan for **F** as a general guide.

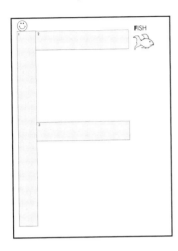 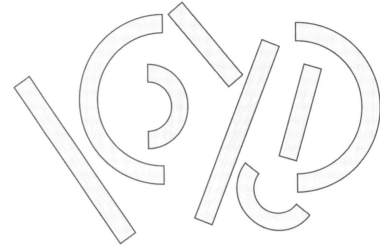

Preparation
Gather Wood Pieces and Letter Cards

Directions
1. Place the **F** card in front of child.
2. Point to the Letter Card. Say, "This is **F**. **F** starts at the ☺. This word is **FISH**. **FISH** begins with **F**."
3. Describe each step as you place the Wood Pieces on the **F**. "I'm getting a big line to start **F**. I'm putting the big line right here, under the ☺. Now, I'm getting a little line to put at the top. There it is. Now, I'm getting another little line to put at the middle. I made **F**."
4. Remove the pieces.

Try this too...
- When working with a group of children, have each one make a different letter. Supervise to be sure the pieces are placed in the correct order. Help students notice the number **1** on the card and then select and place that piece. Follow the numbers to complete each letter correctly.
- When working individually, you may teach planning skills by having a child gather the needed pieces first. Ask, "What do you need to make **F**? First, you need...a big line. How many? One! Get one big line. Then you need...a little line. How many? Two! Get two little lines. You're ready."

Skills Developed
- Letter name for **F**, associating **FISH** with **F**, and **F** sound
- Finding the Wood Pieces for **F** (1 big line, 2 little lines)
- Placing the Wood Pieces correctly (vertical and horizontal)
- Making the letter **F** in the correct sequence of steps

Tips
- Spreading the pieces randomly provides a figure/ground activity. Choosing the correct piece (figure) from the assortment (ground) develops visual discrimination.
- Placing each piece requires fine motor control and spatial (position) awareness. You may help by placing the piece beside the card the way it will be used. Or you may place the piece, take it away, and then let the child try.
- Using cards encourages alphabet awareness. Give each child a card. Have children hold up the cards or line up alphabetically as the letters are called.

Prewriting and Language Skills with Letter Cards

This side of the card has four beginning activities to teach letter awareness and same/different discrimination. Use this lesson plan for **F** as a general guide.

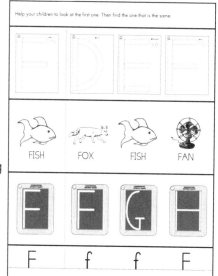

Preparation
1. Gather Wood Pieces and Letter Cards
2. Use the back side of the cards

Directions
Demonstrate Finding the One that Matches
Row 1. Capital letters made with Wood Pieces
Show children how to point to the first letter. Then demonstrate pointing to each letter in turn, looking for the one that matches. For example: Show the card. Say, "This page is about the letter **F**." Point to **F**. Say, "The first letter is **F**. Let's find another **F**."

Point to **D**. Ask, "Is this **F**?...No, no, no. This is **D**. **D** is different."
Point to **E**. Ask, "Is this **F**?...No, no, no. This is **E**. **E** is different."
Point to **F**. Ask, "Is this **F**?...Yes! This is **F**. It is the same letter."

Row 2. Pictures/words that begin with the same capital letter
Show children how to point to the first picture/word. Then demonstrate pointing to each picture/word in turn, looking for the one that matches. Point to **FISH**. Say, "This is a fish. **FISH** starts with **F**. Let's find another fish."

Point to **FOX**. Ask, "Is this a **FISH**? No, no, no. This is a **FOX**."
Point to **FISH**. Ask, "Is this a **FISH**? Yes! This is a **FISH**. It matches."
Point to **FAN**. Ask, "Is this a **FISH**? No, no, no. This is a **FAN**."

Row 3. Capital letters made with chalk on Slates
Find the capital letter that matches the first one.

Row 4. Printed capital and lowercase letters
Find the capital letter that matches the first one.

Skills Developed
- Letter name for **F** and **f**
- Associating **F** with the **FOX**, **FISH**, **FAN**, and the **F** sound
- Same/different concept
- Important habits: Using a page right side up, from top-to-bottom and left-to-right
- Difference between capital **F** and lowercase **f**

Tips
- For children who don't know letters, just do the activity as if you're reading to the child. Encourage participation by following the child's lead.
- Avoid saying "a" or "an" before a letter name. It's confusing to hear "This is a **B**." Simply say, "This is **B**."
- Say "Yes!" enthusiastically and nod your head. Or say "No, no, no" in a cheerful way (like refusing dessert), and shake your head. Children will imitate this.
- The pictures promote left-to-right directionality. See how they face. Move your finger across each row from left to right and encourage children to imitate you.

Capitals with the Mat

Teach children how to make capital letters on the Mat. Unlike the cards, the Mat does not have a letter printed on it. It is simply a bright blue fabric mat (like a mouse pad) with a yellow ☺ in the top left corner.

Preparation
1. Scatter Wood Pieces on the floor in front of children.
2. Give each child a blue Mat.

Demonstrate
Show students how to form the letter piece by piece. Teach in a top-to-bottom, left-to-right order. To see the order for any letter, look in *Letters and Numbers for Me*.

Teacher Demonstrates and Student Imitates Piece by Piece

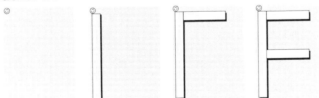

Teach
• When demonstrating, make sure that you make the letter so that it looks right side up from the children's perspective.

What Are We Learning?
• Letter name for **F** (Children like letters they know)
• Finding the Wood Pieces for **F** (one big line and two little lines)
• Making the letter **F** right side up
• Placing the Wood Pieces correctly so **F** is not reversed
• Making the letter **F** in the correct sequence of steps

Tip
• After success with the Mat, teach students with the Slate Chalkboard.

© 2008 Jan Z. Olsen

Other Wood Piece Activities

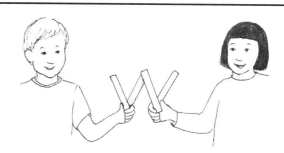

Make Letters Together

Children can have fun holding up Wood Pieces and making letters together. Have them try it. They will have fun figuring out which letters (like the ones that are symmetrical) are easiest to make.

Boss of the Mat

Play *Boss of the Mat*. Students take turns building capital letters on their Mat and guessing one another's letters. The child who is boss gets to tell each child which Wood Piece to pick up next. The boss places one wood piece at a time (the other children follow) until the letter is called out.

Name

The Wood Pieces are a great way to help children learn the letters in their name. Beginners do well writing their name in all capitals. When they are ready, we transition them to title case. For more information on helping children learn to write their names, see page 26 of this guide.

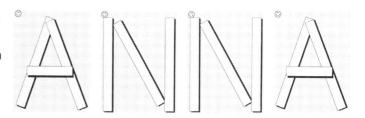

What Letter Is It?

This is a great activity to help children with visual memory. Give the child a Mat with Wood Pieces. Have flash cards prepared with lowercase letters on them. Show students a lowercase letter (on the flashcard) and have them build the capital partner on their mat.

My Turn, Your Turn

Do a tapping activity with two big lines held like an **X**. Teacher taps and students wait to tap until teacher says, "Your turn!" Use just two taps until children learn to listen and wait. When they know how to do this, vary the number or rhythm of taps.

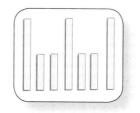

Teacher Says

Play a version of the game Simon Says with the Wood Pieces. Remind your children not to do anything unless you say, "Teacher Says."
Teacher says, "Touch your big line to your nose."

Making Patterns

You can make many patterns using the Wood Pieces. Download these cards with images of Wood Piece patterns. Glue them to heavy card stock and laminate. Set them out in a center and see if children can build patterns to match the cards. This is a great visual activity that helps children learn to follow directions and solve problems.

A Click Away
hwtears.com/click

On the Line

Help children understand basic concepts of letter placement by building words with the Wood Pieces and placing them on a line made out of masking tape. Show children how letters sit right on the line.

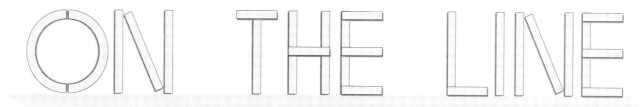

MAT MAN™

Young children often are asked to draw pictures of themselves or a person. Mat Man makes drawing easy. The following Mat Man activities develop a child's body awareness, drawing, and counting skills.

Preparation

Mat
Wood Pieces:
  2 big curves (head)
  3 little curves (ears, mouth)
  4 big lines (arms, legs)
  2 little lines (feet)

Accessories:
  2 hands
  2 eyes (small water bottle caps)
  1 nose (large milk or juice cap)
  other items as desired

Directions for Building and Singing

1. Children sit on the floor in a circle.
2. Teacher builds Mat Man on the floor.
3. Teacher gives Mat Man's parts to the children.
4. Children build Mat Man as they sing the Mat Man song (*Get Set for School Sing Along* CD, Track 8) with the teacher.
5. Extra accessories (belly button, hair, clothing, seasonal items) will make Mat Man more interesting or change him into a different Mat person.

Directions for Drawing

1. Children sit at tables/desks facing teacher. Teacher draws a large Mat Man at the board or easel.
2. Teacher draws each part in order. Sing/ say: "Mat Man has one head. Watch me draw the head. Now it's your turn!"
3. Encourage children to add other details to their drawings.

Skills Developed

- Body Awareness—Body parts, body functions
- Drawing Skills—Placing body parts correctly, sequencing, and organization
- Socialization—Participation, following directions, contributing, taking turns
- Number Awareness—Counting body parts

Tips

- For kindergarteners, demonstrate drawing arms and legs with two parallel lines.
- Encourage students to personalize all of their drawings.
- Children can build Mat Man as they sing and dance to Mat Man, on the *Rock, on the Rock, Rap, Tap & Learn* CD, Track 23.

A Click Away
hwtears.com/click

Personalize Mat Man™

Below is an example of a child who learned Mat Man in preschool and kindergarten. Eventually she learned that Mat Man can be anyone and started to personalize her drawings of people. You can use this activity with your kindergarteners and even help them draw other special people in their lives.

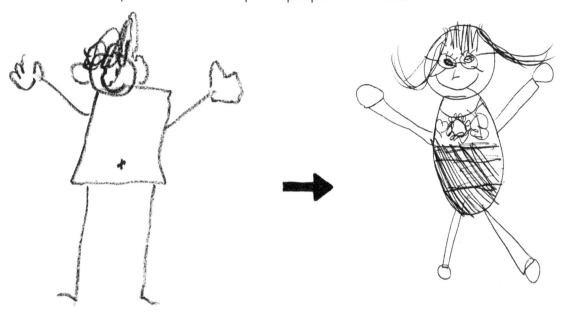

This child's teacher used Mat Man when drawing family portraits. She showed them that girls can have triangles for a dress.

WET-DRY-TRY

Using the Wet–Dry–Try method, your students will learn to form capital letters correctly without reversals. This activity appeals to all learning styles and is a fun way to practice letters.

Slate Chalkboard

Preparation
1. Prepare Slate Chalkboard with the letter you will be teaching.
2. Place Little Chalk Bits and Little Sponge Cubes around the room so children can reach them easily.

Directions

Teacher's Part

Demonstrate correct letter formation.

Student's Part

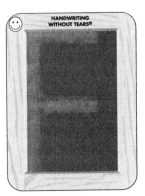

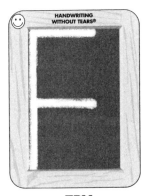

WET
- Wet Little Sponge Cube.
- Squeeze it out.
- Trace the letter with the sponge.
- Wet your finger and trace again.

DRY
- Crumple a little paper towel.
- Dry the letter a few times.
- Gently blow for final drying.

TRY
- Take a Little Chalk Bit.
- Use it to write the letter.

Tips
- Use consistent words to describe the strokes. Match your verbal cues to the directions on the letter lesson pages of the workbook.
- Use Little Sponge Cubes and Little Chalk Bits to help children develop proper pencil grip.
- Squeeze the sponge well or the letter will be too wet.
- This works best one-on-one or in centers with five or fewer students.
- To use this activity with the whole class, pre-mark students' slates with the capital letter (so they have a correct model to wet), and then demonstrate once for everyone.

Other Activities

In addition to doing Wet–Dry–Try with capital letters, you can help children with reversals, names, and more. Below are some easy, fun exercises to get started.

Correcting Reversals
1. Start with a blank slate.
2. Have students copy stroke by stroke the letter/number they will trace.
3. Do Wet–Dry–Try.
3. When you are done, name the letter or number.

What's the secret to preventing the children from using their old habits?
The secret is not naming the letter until the letter is done. Children will copy and practice your way. If you name the letter at the start of the activity, students may skip ahead to their old habits. You'll lose your chance!

Transition Name, Phone Numbers, and Words to paper:
Help children write name, phone number, and words on paper.
1. Prepare slates with students' names or phone numbers.
2. They can Wet–Dry–Try over the numbers.

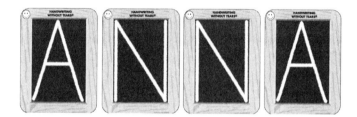

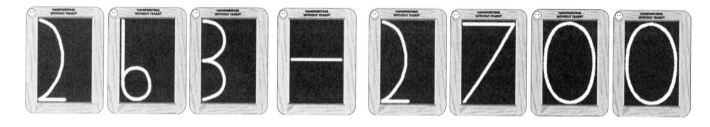

3. Practice on Gray Block Paper.

WET-DRY-TRY

We emphasize correct letter placement because it is essential for neat and fast printing. We teach on double lines to easily impart a sense of how letters should be placed. These Wet–Dry–Try activities on double lines are a great way to teach letter size and place. The image to the right illustrates how we discuss letter size and placement. For additional information, see page 72. Wet–Dry–Try activities appeal to all learning styles and are a fun way to practice letters.

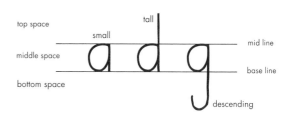

Blackboard with Double Lines

Preparation
1. Prepare Blackboards with Double Lines with the letter you will be teaching.
2. Place Little Chalk Bits and Little Sponge Cubes around the room so children can reach them easily.

Directions

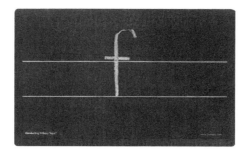

Teacher's Part
Demonstrate correct letter formation.

Student's Part

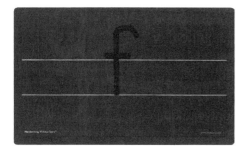
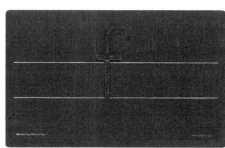
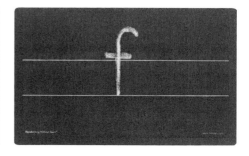

WET	**DRY**	**TRY**
• Wet a Little Sponge Cube.	• Crumple a little paper towel.	• Take a Little Chalk Bit.
• Squeeze it out.	• Dry the letter a few times.	• Use it to write the letter.
• Trace the letter with the sponge.	• Gently blow for final drying.	
• Wet your finger and trace again.		

Tips
- Use consistent words to describe the strokes. Match your verbal cues to the directions on the letter lesson pages of the workbook.
- Use Little Sponge Cubes and Little Chalk Bits. They help children develop proper pencil grip.
- Squeeze the sponge well or the letter will be too wet.
- This works best one-on-one or in centers with five or fewer students.
- To use this activity with the whole class, pre-mark students' chalkboards with the lowercase letter (so they have a correct model to wet), and then demonstrate once for everyone.

Other Blackboard Activities

In addition to doing the Wet–Dry–Try activity with a single lowercase letter, you can help children with bumping the lines, placing letters in words, placing capitals on lines, writing names, and more. Below are some easy, fun exercises to get you started.

Bump the Lines

Help children bump the lines with this simple dot and line exercise.

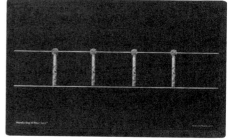

1. Use a piece of chalk to draw 4 to 5 dots with lines across the board.
2. Do the activity just as you would do Wet–Dry–Try with a letter.
3. Have children trace over the lines.
4. Say "bump" when you hit the bottom line.

Try diagonal lines and Magic C strokes too.

Names and Capitalized Words

Demonstrate/Imitate: Title Case (Two Boards)

1. Demonstrate the child's name on one board, as the child imitates on the other.

This activity helps children learn to write their names on double lines before transitioning to paper. Practice writing capital letters and their lowercase partners on the blackboard when you teach the lowercase letter pages.

Word Skills

You can help children learn proper word spacing and letter placement.

1. Point children to the top, middle, and bottom spaces on the board.
2. You can help with word placement by preparing the board with words specific to each space. For example, the word **cows** teaches the middle space. The word **tall** teaches the top space. The word **jog** teaches the bottom space.
3. You can challenge your students by thinking of words with letters that occupy all three spaces. The word **dog** is an example.

DOOR TRACING

Take advantage of the 🙂 by placing it on the door to help children write capitals and numbers. The 🙂 prevents reversals and promotes the top-to-bottom habit.

Expanding Smiley Face Secrets

Preparation
1. Copy, color, cut, and laminate the Smiley Face on the following page.
2. Place it in the top left corner of your classroom door.

Directions
1. While teaching, use your door frame to model letter or number formation for your students.
2. Have children air trace capital letters and numbers on the door.

Skills Developed
This activity gives children extra practice with the orientation, formation, and starting position. Air tracing uses large arm movements for visual and kinesthetic learning.

Tips
Children can trace a letter or number before lunch, recess, or before leaving at the end of the day.
- Consider having a daily or weekly leader who gets to model for the others.
- Use your door to teach parents about HWT Smiley Face secrets.
- Have students partner and play Mystery Letter games with Frog Jump and Magic C capitals.
- Play Boss of the Door. The boss gets to decide which letter or number to trace on the door. A good boss traces well enough so that others can guess the letter.

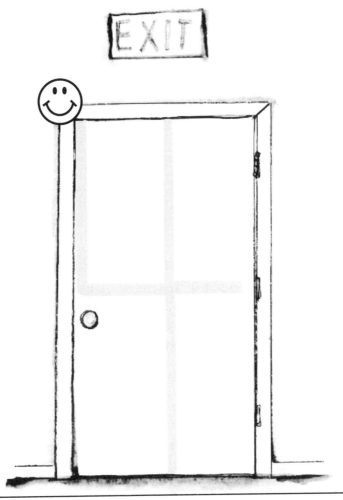

Color, Cut, Laminate, Place

IMAGINARY WRITING

Imaginary writing is a kinesthetic strategy with visual and auditory components. The picking up and holding of pencils adds a tactile component. This strategy allows you to watch the entire class and ensure that all students are making letters correctly.

Air Writing

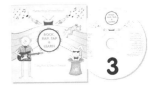

Preparation
Learn *Air Writing*, Track 3, from the *Rock, Rap, Tap & Learn* CD.

Directions
1. Sing to prepare the class for participation.
2. Review a letter or number. Trace it in the air in front of your class.
3. Have students hold a pencil correctly in the air. Everyone checks pencil grips.
4. Retrace the letter or number again with your students.

Tip
If you are facing your students, make the letter backward in relation to you so that the letter will be correct from your students' perspective.

My Teacher Writes

Preparation
Gather chalk or markers for a large board or easel. Use *My Teacher Writes*, Track 21, from the *Rock, Rap, Tap & Learn* CD.

Directions
1. Children sing as you stand in front of the class:
   My teacher writes a letter (number) for me
   What's this letter (number) let's look and see
2. Review a letter or number and trace it in the air or on the board.
3. Have students hold a pencil correctly in the air. Everyone checks pencil grips.
4. Retrace the letter or number again with your students.

Tip
If you are facing your students and doing Air Writing, make the letter backward in relation to you so the letter will be correct from your students' perspective.

Follow the Ball

Preparation
Find a brightly colored cup or ball.

Directions
1. Have students hold a pencil correctly in the air. Everyone checks pencil grips.
2. Face the class and hold up a cup or ball.
3. Have students point their pencils at the cup or ball.
4. Write the letter in the air slowly, giving the directions.
5. Have students follow along with their pencils, saying the directions with you.

Tips
- If you are facing your students, make the letter backward in relation to you so that the letter will be correct from your students' perspective.
- Hold the cup or ball in your right hand, out to your right side at eye level. Stand still.
- Say the steps and letters, perhaps: "Magic c, up like a helicopter, up higher, back down, bump. This is lowercase **d**."

Laser Letters

Preparation
Gather a laser pointer and chalk or markers for a large board or easel.

Directions
1. Write a large letter on a board or easel, giving step-by-step directions.
2. Have students hold a pencil correctly in the air. Everyone checks pencil grips.
3. Move to the back of room, and point the laser to the start of the letter.
4. Have students point their pencils to the laser dot at the start of the letter.
5. Use the laser to trace the letter slowly, giving step-by-step directions.
6. Have students follow with their pencils, saying the directions along with you.

Note: You may decide to allow students to use the laser with your supervision.

Tips
Laser letters are ideal for teaching tricky letters because they enable children to see the following:
- You writing the large letter first
- The laser pointing to the start of the completed letter
- The laser moving along the completed letter

LETTER SIZE AND PLACE: THE HAND ACTIVITY

Teaching children the correct size and placement of letters is one of the most important things you can do to help make their printing neat and fast. The simple hand activity below is fun, gets the students' attention, and is a great way to help children learn the concepts of letter size and place. Students will develop a sense for how letters fit relative to one another, enabling them to write letters the correct size and put them in the correct vertical place.

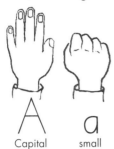 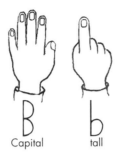 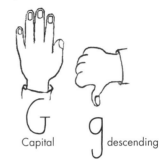

Capital   small   Capital   tall   Capital   descending

Capital letters – Left hand
- Make a flat hand for all capitals.

Capital

A B C D E F G H I J K L M N O P Q R S T U V W X Y Z

Lowercase letters – Right hand
- Make a fisted hand for small letters.
- Point the index finger up for tall letters.
- Point the thumb down for descending letters.

 Small   a c e i m n o r s u v w x z   **Tall**   b d f h k l t   **Descending**   g j y p q

Directions
1. Demonstrate capitals by holding up your flat hand.
2. Demonstrate lowercase by holding up your hand for a small, tall, or descending letter.
3. Call out a letter, write it on the board, and show the hand position.

Note: Don't use this activity for children learning sign language because it may create confusion.

Directions for Hand Positions for Letters on the Board
1. Write the first lowercase letter.
2. Ask students if the first letter is small, tall, or descending.
3. Students make the right hand show the answer: small, tall, or descending. Do each letter in the word.

Alternately, write the complete word and have the class do hand positions as you say each letter.

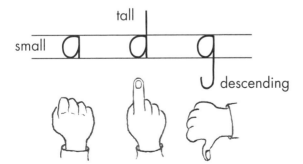 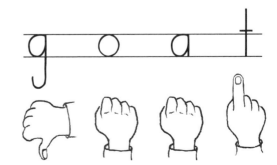

VOICES

Even with the child-friendly language in the HWT program, the steps for forming letters can get a little boring. Repeating step-by-step directions using different voices makes it fun and really helps solidify the steps in students' minds.

Preparation

1. Pre-mark the double lines on the chalkboard.
2. Begin at the far left of the board.
3. Have students open their workbooks to find the step-by-step directions for forming the letter you have chosen.

Directions

Magic c   up like a   bump   back down bump

1. Demonstrate the letter formation step-by-step.
2. Say the words that are in the workbook, and ask children to say the words with you.
3. Repeat the activity using the following voices:
   - **high**
   - **low**
   - **loud**
   - **soft**
   - **slow**
   - **fast**

Tips

- Allow your students to pick the voice for the class to use. Make it even more fun by trying voices that are spooky, shaky, robotic, etc.
- Teach with voices using the Magic C Bunny by having the bunny whisper in your ear the voice the children should use.

MYSTERY LETTERS

You can play Mystery Letters with children as a fun way to develop good habits. Mystery Letter lessons are for teaching correct letter formation. The secret is making the first stroke correctly before telling children the name of the letter they're going to make. This ensures that students start the letter correctly and consistently.

CAPITAL MYSTERIES

Preparation

1. Gather Slates, Little Chalk Bits, and paper towels for erasing.
2. Say the directions as indicated below.

Directions

For **F E D P B R N M**
Start in the starting corner
Big line down
Frog jump to the starting corner
Now make ____

For **H K L**
Start in the starting corner
Big line down
Now make ____

For **U V W X Y Z**
Start in the starting corner
Now make ____

For **C O Q G**
Start at the top center
Make a Magic C
Now make ____

For **S A I T J**
Start at the top center
Now make ____

Play Mystery Game for Frog Jump Capitals

Play the Mystery Letter game to reinforce correct habits for Frog Jump Capitals (page 17 in *Letters and Numbers for Me*). The game is fun and teaches children to use correct habits. Students start at the top and don't make reversals. Here's how to play:

1. Tell students to put the pencil on the starting corner dot and make a big line down.
2. Tell them to frog jump back to the starting corner dot and wait.
3. Call out a mystery letter, one of the Frog Jump Capitals, for them to make.

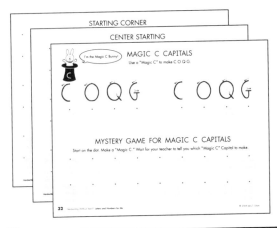

Play More Mystery Games

Play Mystery Letter games to reinforce correct habits for Starting Corner and Center Starting capitals. You can play these games on Gray Block Paper.

For Magic C Capitals, turn to page 32 in *Letters and Numbers for Me*.
- Allow children to use colored pencils to make their letters.
- Use the Magic C puppet to tell the children the Mystery Letter.
- See page 103 of this guide for detailed directions.

Lowercase Mysteries

Preparation

1. Gather Blackboard with Double Lines, Little Chalk Bits, and paper towels for erasing.
2. Say the directions as indicated below.
3. Optional: For children who need extra help, you can make the first stroke for them to trace.

Directions
Magic C Letters

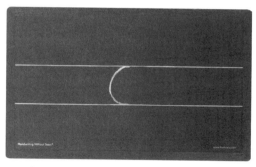

For letters **a d g o q**
Magic c, wait. Turn it into _____.

Magic C Words

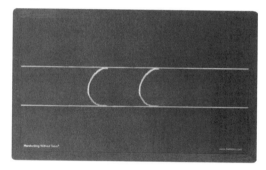

Using **a d g o q**
Magic c, wait, turn it into _____.
Add letter _____.

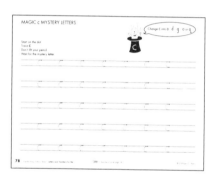

Turn to page 78 in *Letters and Numbers for Me.*
• Allow children to use colored pencils to make their letters.
• Use the Magic C Bunny to tell the children the mystery letter.
• See page 141 of this guide for detailed directions.

Other Lowercase Letters

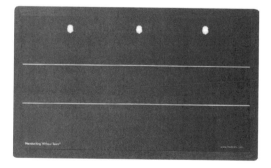

For letters **h b k l t**
Start up high, make a big line down, wait. Turn it into _____.

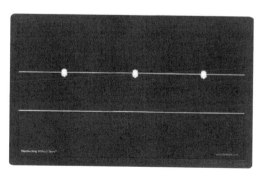

For letters **i j m n p r s u v w x y z**
Start at the dot. Make _____.

LETTER STORIES

Fun stories help children remember letters that are a bit tricky. Beyond our simple verbal cues, we made up some stories that are fun to share and help make these letters memorable.

b

Honeybee
Say, "Let's make letter **h**. Now let's make another **h**. I have a surprise. This is an **h** for a honeybee." Turn **h** into **b**.

e

Run the bases
Place the pencil on the dot. Say, "Batter up to bat. Here comes the pitch. Hit the ball, wait, then run the bases: first, second, third, Stop! It's not a home run."

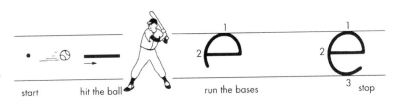

start   hit the ball   run the bases   stop

f

Fire hose squirts
Say, "**f** is like water squirting out of a fire hose. It goes up and then falls down."

g

If George falls
Say, "Inside **g** lives a little man named George (draw a little face in **g**)." He says, "Ohhhh, if I fall, will you catch me?" Say, "Sure, I will catch you (turn the **g** to catch George) if you fall."

Ohhhh, if I fall, will you catch me?

Teacher says, "Sure, I will catch you if you fall."

k

Karate K
Say, "The big line is Mr. Kaye, your karate teacher. He wants you to show him your kick. Put the pencil on the line. That's you. Now kick Mr. Kaye. Hiiii-ya. That's the karate **k**."

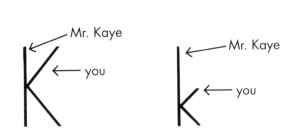

Mr. Kaye   Mr. Kaye
you   you

m

Stinky m

Say, "If **m** has a big gap, people will throw trash in the gap. Don't make a big gap. Make the gap so little, there is only room for an upside down chocolate kiss."

q

U-turn

Say, "The letter **q** is followed by **u**.
Think of quiet, quit, quibble, quaint, etc.
At the bottom of **q**, stop and make a **u**-turn."

S

Stop, Drop, and Roll with S

Start **s** with a little **c**. Then what do you do if your clothes catch on fire? You stop, drop, and roll!

 Go over and say hello to the smiley face.

 Stop, drop, and roll.

Tt

T is tall, t is tall but...

Look at me. I can make capital **T**.
Look at me. I can make lowercase **t**.
Capital **T** is tall.
Lowercase **t** is tall, but it's crossed lower.
Capital **T** and lowercase **t** are both tall.

Z

Z chase

Left hand says, "I'm going to chase you."
Right hand picks up the pencil and runs across the
page. Left hand says, "I'm kidding! Come back."
Right hand slides back down toward the left hand.
Left hand says, "Ha! I'm going to chase you."
Right hand runs back across.

(This activity is for right-handers with z reversal problems, but can be adapted for lefties)

POSTURE, PAPER, AND PENCIL SKILLS
PREPARING FOR PAPER AND PENCIL

When it comes to handwriting, children must be taught everything! That includes how to sit, position paper, and hold a pencil. This is the physical approach to handwriting. Sometimes it's the physical approach, not the letters and numbers, that causes a child to have trouble with handwriting. Think of it as playing a musical instrument. If you don't know how to position yourself and hold the instrument correctly, how can you play beautiful music? The same is true with writing letters and numbers. The ability to position yourself and hold your pencil correctly has a lot to do with being able to write legibly.

The important questions are:
- How do you get children to sit up while writing?
- How do you position the paper?
- What is the secret to a good pencil grip?

As you'll see in the next few pages...

Posture: Good Posture Can Be Fun

Does the furniture fit? The right size and style chair and desk affect school performance. Children don't come in a standard size! Check that every child can sit with feet flat on the floor and arms resting comfortably. Children who sit on their feet often will lose stability in their upper torso. On the following page we show you how good posture can be fun. We have a secret for getting children to stop sitting on their feet.

Paper: Place the Paper

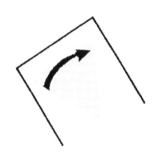

There's a misperception that people should slant their paper to make slanted writing. Not true. In fact, we slant paper so that it fits the natural arc of the forearm. Children who slant their papers properly can write faster because the arm moves naturally with the paper.

Pencil Skills: Grasping Grip

The most important thing to understand about pencil grip is that it doesn't develop naturally; it is learned. Based on our years of experience helping children, we developed our own theories about how to develop good pencil grip habits effectively. Because children are born imitators, demonstration will lead to success.

On the next few pages, we explain fun strategies to help you teach posture, paper, and pencil skills.

GOOD POSTURE CAN BE FUN
Arms and Hands

Here are some warm-ups that children enjoy.

Push palms

Pull hands

Hug yourself tightly

Total Posture – Stomp!

Stomping is fun and really works! Students' feet will be on the floor and parallel in front of them. The arm movements make their trunks straight. The noise and chaos let them release energy, but it's under your control. When you have them stop stomping, they'll have good posture and be ready to pay attention. Use stomping a few times a day.

Directions

1. Sit down and show the children how to stomp their feet and wave their arms in the air.
2. Have them shout, "Na, na, naaah, na, na, naaah," with you as they wave and stomp.

The Stomping Game

Use *Stomp Your Feet*, Track 10, from the *Rock, Rap, Tap & Learn* CD.

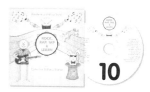

Directions

1. Children push their chairs away from their desks to get ready.
2. Sing and follow along with the music and movement.

Head and Shoulders

Do this activity any time you find your children sagging.

Raise shoulders up

Pull shoulders back

Let them down

PLACE THE PAPER

Where's the paper? Most children naturally place a bowl of ice cream in front of them. However, they may lean way over in awkward positions to write. Children who put their paper in front of them and slant it properly can write faster because they position their arms naturally with the paper. You need to teach them how to place their papers appropriately. Have them turn to page 6 in *Letters and Numbers for Me*, and teach them how to slant their papers appropriately for their handedness.

Children who can print sentences across the page are ready to tilt the paper at a slight angle to follow the natural arc of the writing hand. The correct way to tilt the paper is easy to remember (see the illustrations below). For right-handed children, put the right corner higher; for left-handed children, put the left corner higher. The writing hand is below the line of writing. This practice encourages the correct neutral wrist position.

Left–Handed Students   **Right-Handed Students**

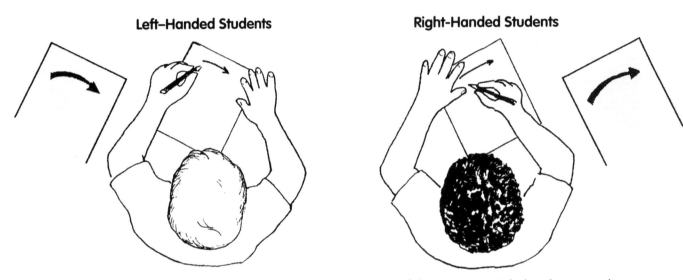

- **Left–Handed Children** tend to exaggerate the position of their papers. It helps them see their writing. For more information on left-handed children, turn to page 66.
- **Beginners** who are learning to print letters and words should place the paper straight in front of them.

Tip
- Sometimes children need reminders about how to place their paper. Draw an arrow on the bottom corner (bottom left corner for right-handed children, bottom right corner for left-handed children). Tell them to point the arrow to their belly button.

Left   **Right**

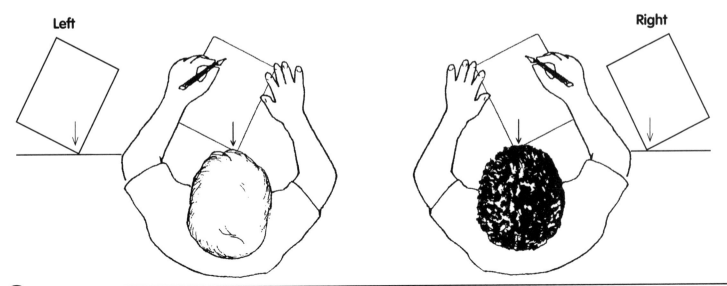

GRASPING GRIP

Educators all have questions about pencil grip. We are frequently asked why awkward pencil grips happen and how to correct them. We seldom hear about how to prevent them. A good pencil grip does not develop naturally. In fact, several factors affect how a child learns to hold a pencil correctly.

Below is our top 10 list of the things we often think about regarding grip:

Experiences

We develop pencil grip habits while we are young. Children who are encouraged to feed themselves have more fine motor experiences than those who are spoon fed. Children who have early self-feeding experiences may have an easier time learning how to hold their crayons and pencils.

Toys

Today's toys are very different from those with which we grew up. We should always encourage and remind parents about non-battery operated toys, which help build hand strength.

Imitation

Children are born imitators. When they are watching you write, always demonstrate a correct grip because they tend to do as you do.

Early Instruction

Help children place their fingers. Teach preschoolers and kindergarteners their finger names and finger jobs and show them how their fingers should hold writing tools.

Tool Size

Choose appropriate writing tools. We prefer small tools: Little Sponge Cubes, Little Chalk Bits, FLIP Crayons™, and Pencils for Little Hands. These tools promote using the finger tips naturally. Large tools elicit a fisted grip; small tools, a more mature grip. As adults, we write with pencils that are in proportion to our hands. Shouldn't children do the same?

Timing

It is difficult to correct the grips of older children because we have to re-teach them motor patterns. Old habits die hard. Older children need time to get used to a new way of holding a pencil. It takes repetition, persistence, and practice.

Blanket Rules

Avoid blanket rules about pencil grip devices. Some devices may work for a child. If they are motivating and work, use them. You should save these devices as a last resort and use them for older children who understand their purpose.

Acceptance

Some awkward pencil grips are functional. If the child is comfortable and doesn't have speed or legibility issues, let it go.

Joints

We are all made differently. Some of us have joints that are more relaxed. Therefore, expect slight variations in what would be considered a standard grip. If a child is unable to use a standard grip, you may consider an altered grip as illustrated. The pencil is placed between the index and middle fingers.

Summer

This is the perfect time to change an awkward grip. Take advantage of the child's down time to create new habits.

The Correct Grip

The standard way for children to hold their pencil is illustrated below. If you write using a grip that is different than tripod or quadropod, alter your grip for classroom demonstration.

Tripod Grip
Thumb, Index Finger, Middle Finger

Quadropod Grip
Thumb, Index Finger, Middle Finger, Ring Finger

 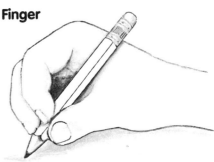

A Note About Pencil Size

Start by using golf size pencils in kindergarten and first grade. As children gain handwriting experience, their control will improve. At that time, transition them to a standard size pencil.

Sing *Picking Up My Pencil*

Use this song from the *Rock, Rap, Tap & Learn* CD to make your pencil grip lessons more memorable. Children will know the tune *Baby Bumble Bee*. You sing the first verse; they'll join in the second.

Directions
1. Listen to Track 9 as background music a few times with your students.
2. For fun, review the names of the fingers: thumb, pointer, tall man (middle finger).
3. Without the CD, sing and demonstrate verse one.
4. Children will then get ready by picking up their pencils, checking their own and their neighbor's grip, and joining you to sing the second verse.

*The fast pace of the song is to encourage teachers and children to pick up the tune quickly and to inspire them to sing it on their own.

The tips shown here will help your students hold the pencil with the right combination of mobility and control. These exercises make it easy and fun for children to learn a correct pencil grip.

A-OK

Right-handed

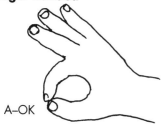

A–OK

drop fingers

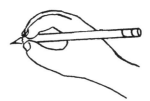

open

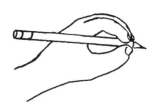

Step 1.	**Step 2.**	**Step 3.**
Make the A-OK sign.	Drop the fingers. Open the A-OK.	Pinch the pencil.

Left-handed

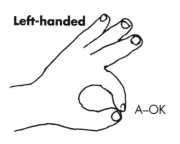

A–OK

drop fingers

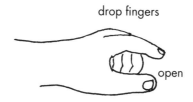

open

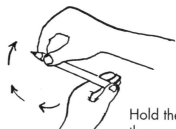

Flip the Pencil Trick

Here is another method. It is a trick that someone introduced to us at a workshop. It's such fun that we love to share it. Children like to do it and it puts the pencil in the correct position. (Illustrated for right-handed students.)

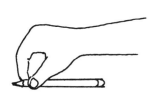

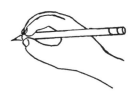

Place pencil on table pointing away from you. Pinch the pencil on the paint where the paint meets the wood.

Hold the eraser and twirl the pencil around.

Voila! Correct grip.

Pencil Pick-Ups

We created these fun Pencil Pick-Ups for children to practice their pencil grips. Think of it as a pencil warm-up. Turn to page 7 of *Letters and Numbers for Me*. Have children do one item of their choice. Don't forget to say "drop 'em" in between pictures. Children will drop their pencils, pick them up, and choose another pencil pick-up.

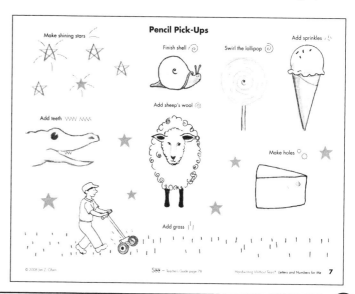

For more grip activities and pencil pick-ups, visit **www.hwtears.com/click**

LOOKING OUT FOR LEFTIES

Many wonder if left-handed children require different instruction than right-handed child. In fact, you instruct them the same way, with a few exceptions. Because our world typically favors the right-handed population, worksheets and letter sequence charts usually don't make special considerations. We have tips for teaching left-handed children that will prevent bad habits and make handwriting easier.

Preventing a Poor Wrist Position

Typical Worksheet		
Write the word	Write the word again	Write the word again
1. truck	truck	truck
air		
school		
usher		
taste		
8. drink		

The child can't see a model.

Worksheet		
Write the word again	Write the word again
truck	truck	truck
2. grab		
3. bull		
4. chair		
5. school		
6. usher		
7. taste		
8. drink		

Child accommodates but ends up in a bad position.

Many worksheets list things on just the left side. Left-handed children struggle with this format because their hand covers the thing they are attempting to copy. To accommodate their situation, some left-handed individuals will hook their wrist to see what it is they are supposed to write. After a while, the movement becomes so automatic that some children develop a natural hooked wrist pattern. This type of writing can be uncomfortable and tiring.

You can prevent this problem by photocopying the child's worksheet/workbook page and placing it to the right for the child to reference for copying.

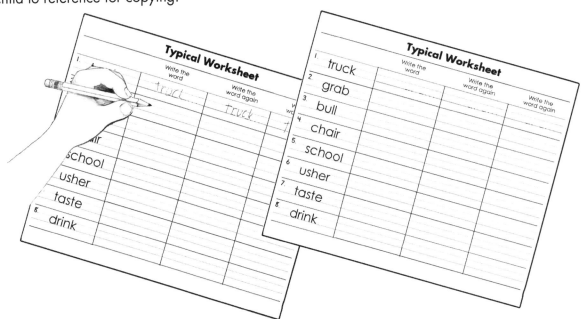

Give another copy of the worksheet to the child so the model can be seen.

Left-Hand Friendly Worksheets

When creating your own worksheets, you can make them right- and left-hand friendly in two ways:

1. Have the child copy below the model.

2. Place the word to be copied in the middle of the page.

İS

İS

Paper Placement

You might observe some left-handed children slanting their papers too much. They do this to prevent their wrists from hooking. You can allow them to exaggerate the slant on their papers if it doesn't cause speed or neatness trouble.

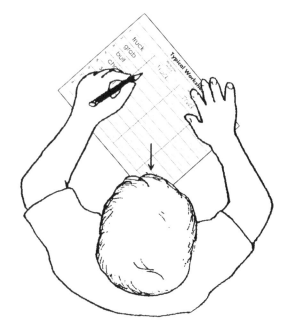

Cross Strokes

Mark arrows → for right-handed students. Mark arrows ← for left-handed students.

A E Ff G H I J Tt

When writing letters and numbers, we typically travel top-to-bottom, left-to-right. At times, left-handed children will choose to pull into their writing hand from right to left. Allow left handed children to cross by pulling into their hand. Model it for them in their workbooks.

Why Children (and Teachers) Succeed with HWT

HWT LETTER AND NUMBER STYLE

HWT uses a simple, continuous, vertical stroke that is easy to learn. The HWT letter style is also familiar because it looks like the letters and words children see and read every day. The continuous stroke style prevents reversals and prepares children for a smooth transition to cursive.

Aa Bb Cc Dd Ee Ff Gg Hh Ii Jj Kk Ll Mm
Nn Oo Pp Qq Rr Ss Tt Uu Vv Ww Xx Yy Zz

1 2 3 4 5 6 7 8 9

Advantages of the HWT Style
- Follows developmental principles
- Enables ease of reading and writing
- Prevents reversals
- Looks and feels child friendly
- Features letter models with an appealing, handwritten quality

Vertical print uses 4 simple shapes.
1. Vertical lines
2. Horizontal lines
3. Circles and curves
4. Diagonal lines

Slanted print uses 12 different strokes.
Slanted print is difficult to describe and developmentally more difficult to master.

Vertical print is simple and straight.

Not Reversible

Slanted print has tails or fancy endings.
With tails, these letters are asymmetrical, leading to more reversals.

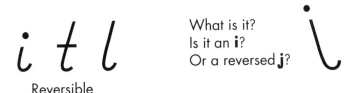

Reversible

What is it?
Is it an **i**?
Or a reversed **j**?

Vertical print is neater and holds up better in use. There is no advantage to using a slanted style for printing. Despite claims to the contrary, slanted print does not make the transition to cursive easier. The HWT continuous stroke style is ideal for printing and transitioning to cursive.

UNIQUE WORKBOOK FEATURES
Large Step-By-Step Illustrated Directions
It is so much easier for children to understand how to form letters if you show them how step-by-step. Other programs show a completed letter with a bunch of tiny arrows pointing the way around the letter. It is very difficult for a child to learn how to write that way. Step-by-step is the way to letter formation success.

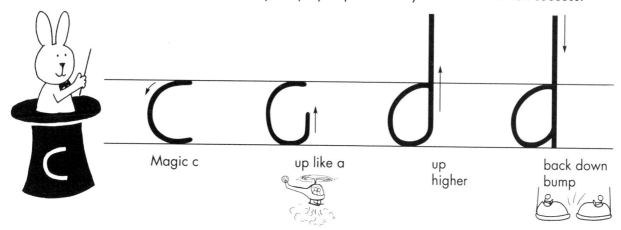

Magic c   up like a   up higher   back down bump

Child-Friendly Consistent Terminology
HWT's child-friendly language evolved in response to other programs' complicated letter terminology. When teaching letters to children, HWT doesn't assume they fully understand left/right orientation, clockwise/counter clockwise, or forward/backward. That complex terminology is confusing and unnecessary. HWT makes it easy by using fewer words and only words that children already know and understand.

HWT is simple for children to comprehend.

HWT Language:
Magic c
up like a helicopter
up higher
back down
bump

Take a look at what other programs say to form **d**:

Example 1:
Middle start; around down, touch, up high, down, and a monkey tail.

Example 2:
Touch below the midline; circle back (left all the way around). Push up straight to the headline. Pull down straight to the baseline.

Pencil Pick-Ups Encourage Grip Practice
Pencil Pick-Ups are designed to encourage children to hold their pencils correctly while doodling. They are a perfect warm-up activity that enables teachers to teach and check pencil grip. The Pencil Pick-Ups are on page 7 of *Letters and Numbers for Me*.

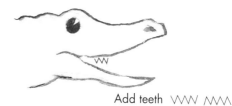

Add teeth ᐯᐯᐯ ᐱᐱᐱ

Capitals in Gray Blocks
Gray Blocks and starting dots help children control the size and shape of their capitals. Gray Blocks also prevent reversals. Here's how:

F E D P B R N M H K L start on the dot in the top left (starting corner) with a big line down. When that line is on the left side, the next part is always on the right side. No reversals!

U V W X Y Z start in the starting corner, too.

The dot in the top center is the place to begin:
C O Q G S A I T J
Starting at the top is the most important handwriting habit. The dot at the top teaches children to begin there automatically.

Copy Just One Model at a Time

Have you seen papers or workbooks that require children to copy a letter over and over across the page? The child copies the model and then copies the copy of the model, and so on. The letters get progressively worse. It's boring. Ideally, the child should make just one letter beside each model.

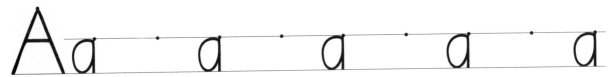

Continuous Meaningful Review

Children retain skills better if they have continuous, meaningful review. That's why each new letter is used in words and sentences that emphasize practice of the new letter and help children review and practice previously learned letters.

Room to Write

When children are learning to print, they need extra room to write. Because they can't print with the precision of machines, they cram their words to make them fit into spaces that are too small. HWT workbooks give them the room they need to write.

HWT models good spacing and gives plenty of room to write to help children develop good spacing habits.

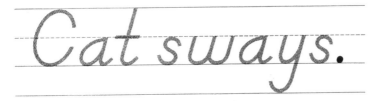

Other programs give poor spacing models and inadequate room for writing. Children are expected to make letters with the precision of a professional graphic designer at a keyboard.

Example 1:

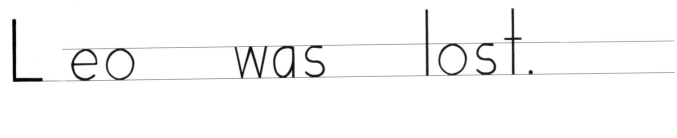

Example 2:

Cat sways.

Left-Hand Friendly Design

The HWT workbooks are left-hand friendly. Every page places the models so that left-handed children can easily see the model they are copying. Lefties never have to lift their hands or place them in an awkward position to see a model. We give models on the right side so that when a left-handed child's arm covers the left aligned models, they can still see a model to copy.

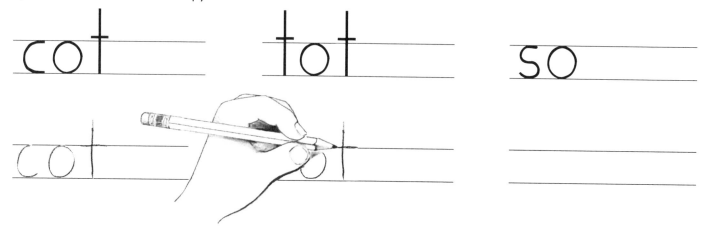

Simple Black-and-White Pages

Our workbooks have black-and-white pages that are clean and clear. We deliberately avoid the visual confusion of distracting background images, overdone colored graphics, multicolored lines, and crowded pages. These fancy effects can create visual perception difficulties for children and distract them.

The simple workbook pages keep children happy and occupied. Children who finish ahead of others can color the pictures or add drawings to the pages.

Children enjoy seeing their own writing and coloring or drawing on the pages. They like the handwritten models, which look more like their own writing. Our workbooks celebrate the child's work.

Left-to-Right Directionality

This is an exciting, unique feature of the HWT workbooks. Look at our illustrations. They promote left-to-right directionality. The car, helicopter, horse, and other drawings are going left to right across the page to encourage correct visual tracking and writing direction.

Fair Practice

In the workbooks, we never ask the child to copy or use a letter that has not yet been taught. The words and sentences use only the letters that the children already know. Using unfamiliar letters for instructional practice is unfair and causes children to develop bad habits.

Teaching Reversal Free Numbers

We begin by teaching numbers with the Gray Blocks, which are like pictures of the Slate Chalkboard. The Gray Blocks prevent reversals and help children learn to place the numbers. Our simple numbers and teaching strategies produce numbers that are reversal-proof.

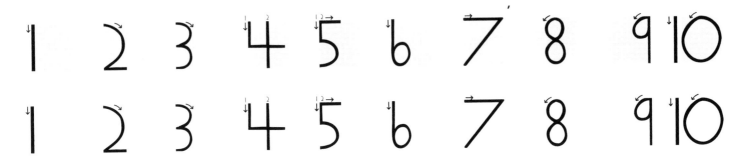

- We teach the numbers in numerical order.
- **1 2 3 4 5 6 7** begin in the top left (starting) corner.
- **8** starts at the top, but in the center.
- **9** starts at the top, but in the right corner.
- **10** is made with **1** and **O** (Number **O** and letter **O** are made the same way.)

Each number page also gives a review of previously learned numbers. The children practice writing numbers on Gray Blocks and on a single line.

Double Lines and Other Lines

With so many lines and so many styles, children need paper that will prepare them for it all. HWT Double Lines teach children to place letters correctly and naturally. With just two lines, children understand quickly how to place letters. Small letters fit in the middle space. Tall letters go into the top space. Descending letters go into the bottom space. Later students can apply that philosophy to other styles of paper they'll get in school. We also give them practice with other lines along the way.

Take a look at space.

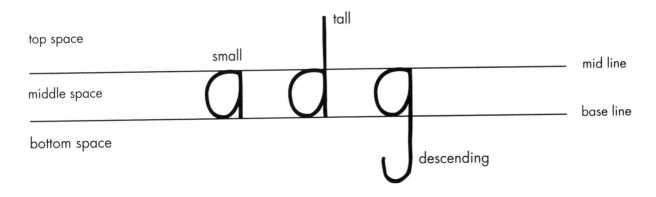

Line Generalization: Success on All Paper Styles

In *Letters and Numbers for Me*, we provide activities for children to experience different types of lined paper. Practice using simple double lines makes it easy for students to succeed on any style of paper.

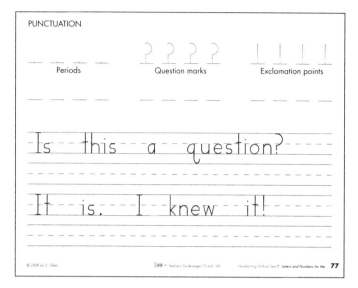

Line Generalization Success

This child's sample shows line transition skills from HWT double lines to a journal entry with triple lines.

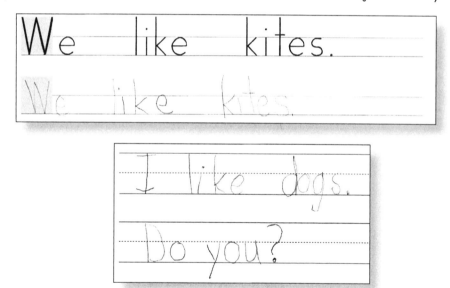

Paper Quality

Who would have thought that the quality of paper could affect handwriting? We tested all kinds of paper and we know good paper when we see it. Our handwriting paper is selected based on the following qualities:

1. **Writability** – This is referred to as tooth. When paper has good tooth, you can actually hear the pencil. Paper with tooth gives children feedback and assists with control. Smooth paper doesn't have tooth. It is hard to write on.

2. **Erasability** – Nothing is worse than paper that won't erase or paper that wrinkles and tears. Sturdy paper withstands erasing.

3. **Opacity** – We have the thickest sheets with the most opacity to reduce the amount of see through.

4. **Brightness** – Our paper is white. This paper helps a child's work stand out.

Letters and Numbers for Me
WHAT'S IN THE WORKBOOK

Letters and Numbers For Me is divided into three major sections—capitals, lowercase letters, and numbers. In the workbook, you'll find Words for Me and Sentences for Me. These pages give children the opportunity to practice their new letters in fun language arts activities that are age appropriate.

Capital Letter and Word Pages

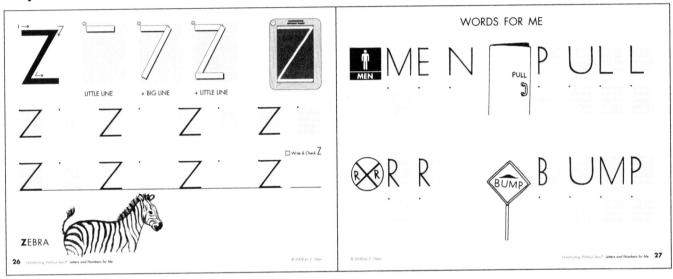

- Pages show large step-by-step instructions for letter formation with Wood Pieces and on the Slate.
- ☑ Check letter teaches children to self-edit their work.
- Capital letters are reinforced with real world examples of capitals.

Lowercase Letter, Word, and Sentence Pages

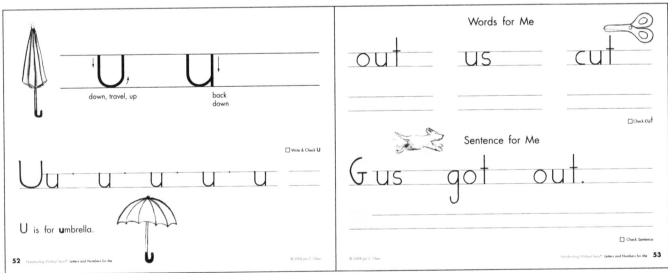

- Newly taught letters are used in practice words and sentences.
- ☑ Check word teaches children self-editing skills.
- Good spacing is modeled.
- ☑ Check Sentence teaches children self-editing skills.

Activity Pages

- Activity pages reinforce the handwriting lessons while supporting other language arts lessons.

- Children learn to write words, poems, and paragraphs.

- Children learn to write on paper with different line styles.

- Lessons are fun and engaging for students.

Number Pages

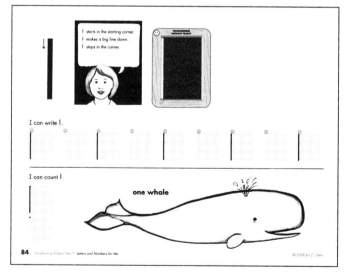

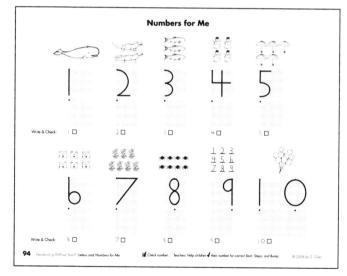

- Numbers are reviewed in Gray Blocks to prevent reversals.
- Fun stories accompany step-by-step number instruction.
- Review pages are functional and provide counting practice.

WHAT YOU WILL TEACH...

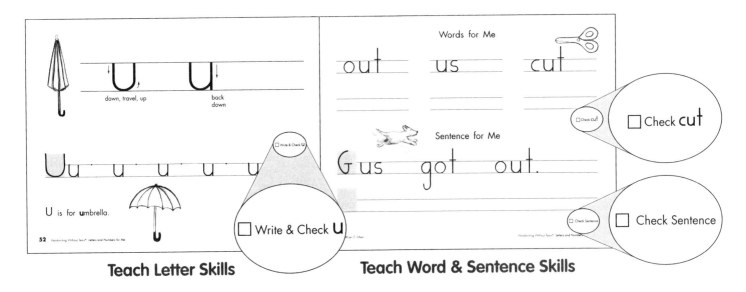

Teach Letter Skills **Teach Word & Sentence Skills**

Letter Skills

Children need to know exactly how to make letters. Teach them and tell them:

1. Start correctly.
2. Do each step.
3. Bump the lines.

Use multisensory instruction for teaching letter formation. Children enjoy learning with different Voices on page 55 of this guide and Wet–Dry–Try on the Blackboard with Double Lines, page 48.

Word Skills

There are three steps to writing words well:

1. Make letters the correct size.
2. Place letters correctly – tall, small, or descending.
3. Put letters close.

Use the Hand Activity, page 54 of this guide, to help children understand letter size and placement.
How close should the letters be? Very close. Have children put their index fingers very close together, but not touching. That close!

Sentence Skills

Sentences must:

1. Start with a capital.
2. Put space between words.
3. End with . ? or !

This is easy and fun. There's even a *Sentence Song*, Track 7, on the *Rock, Rap, Tap & Learn* CD. Sing it to *Yankee Doodle*.

...AND HOW THEY WILL CHECK

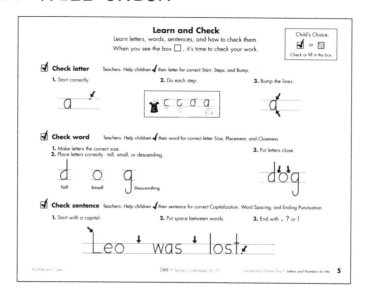

✅ **Check letter** Teachers: Help children ✓ their letter for correct Start, Steps, and Bump.

1. Start correctly.　　　　　　　**2.** Do each step.　　　　　　　**3.** Bump the lines.

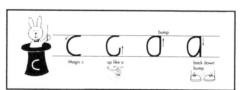

✅ **Check word** Teachers: Help children ✓ their word for correct letter Size, Placement, and Closeness.

1. Make letters the correct size.　　　　　　　　　**3.** Put letters close.
2. Place letters correctly—tall, small, or descending.

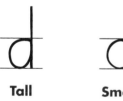

Tall　　**Small**　　**Descending**

✅ **Check sentence** Teachers: Help children ✓ their sentence for correct Capitalization, Word Spacing, and Ending Punctuation.

1. Start with a capital.　　　**2.** Put space between words.　　　**3.** End with **.** **?** or **!**

WARM-UPS

Teach Pencil Pick-Ups

Get Started Say, "Turn to page 7. We are going to warm-up our fingers and practice holding our pencils. Let's pick up our pencils (walk around the room and check grip). I'm checking your fingers, now drop your pencils and let's do it again (check grips again). Now you are ready with a perfect pencil grip. Choose a picture on the page that you want to finish."

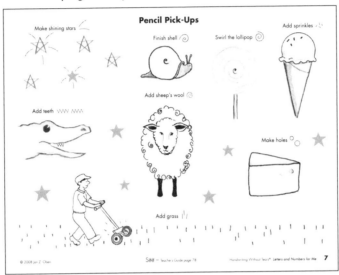

Multisensory Activities

Music and Movement
Use the *Rock, Rap, Tap & Learn* CD.
Play *Picking Up My Pencil*, Track 9.
See page 30 of this guide.

About this Page
Holding the pencil correctly is a good habit that will serve your children for years. Even if they come to you with awkward or inefficient grips, you can help them build new habits this year. This page will help you.

Tell Them...
This is such a fun page. There's so much to do. Do you see something you'd like to do? Add sprinkles to the ice cream cone? Add holes to the cheese? This Pencil Pick-Ups page has fun things to do. We are going to do a little bit on this page today, tomorrow, and for many more days.

How do I teach this?
Prepare for this page by helping children find the grip that suits them on page 6 of the workbook.
1. First identify which is the writing hand: left or right.
2. Then decide which grip is to be used: tripod or quadropod.
3. Have children mark the grip illustration that is correct for them.
   - Circle it
   - Color it
Demonstrate on the board a few sample Pencil Pick-Up strokes: stars, holes, grass, or teeth.
Do a two-step lesson over a period of several days:
1. Pick up a pencil and hold it in the air to check that it's the correct grip.
2. Make marks for just a few seconds—about five—then stop, drop the pencil, and repeat.
Go on to a letter lesson page.

CAPITALS

Teach Frog Jump Capitals F E D P B R N M

Get Started   Say, "Turn to page 8. We are going to start with the Frog Jump Capitals. See how the frog made capital **F**. After the big line, he had to frog jump back to the starting corner. We are going to learn and write Frog Jump Capitals."

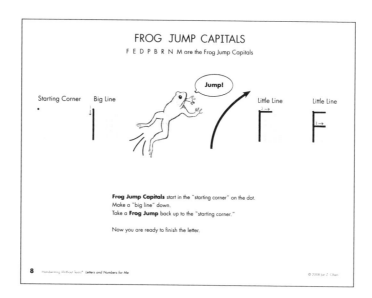

Multisensory Activities

Music and Movement
Use the *Rock, Rap, Tap & Learn* CD, *Frog Jump Letters*, Track 12. While standing, finger trace Frog Jump Capitals in the air. Let children jump between the letters.

Teach the Frog Jump Capitals

Frog Jump Capitals start in the starting corner on the dot. Have children point to the first Gray Block. The Gray Block is like a picture of the slate. There is a dot in the top left corner, the starting corner.

1. Big line down.
   Look at the next Gray Block. There is a big line. The big line goes down from the starting corner and stops in the bottom corner.
2. Frog Jump!
   The frog jumps back up to the starting corner. It's time to finish the letter.
3. Little line across top, little line across middle
   The letter is finished (Capital **F**).

Tips
- Encourage students to say the directions out loud. Children like to say "ribbit" for the frog jump.
- Notice that when the starting line is on the left edge of the Slate or Gray Block, the next part of the letter must be placed on the right side. No reversals!

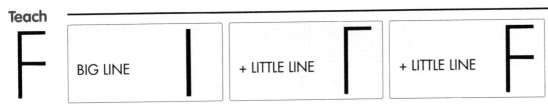

F | BIG LINE | I | + LITTLE LINE | Γ | + LITTLE LINE | F

Get Started Say, "Turn to page 9. This is capital **F**. Watch me write capital **F**. I make it like this (demonstrate). Let's read this word: **FISH**."

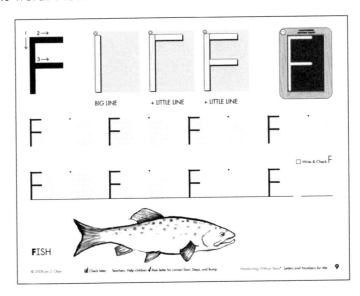

Multisensory Activities

Music and Movement

Use the *Rock, Rap, Tap & Learn* CD, *Frog Jump Letters*, Track 12. While standing, finger trace Frog Jump Capitals in the air. Let children jump between the letters.

Wood Pieces
See page 42 of this guide.

Wet–Dry–Try
See page 46 of this guide.

Finger Trace Models Step-by-Step

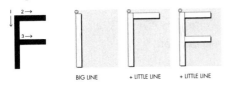

BIG LINE + LITTLE LINE + LITTLE LINE

Say the step-by-step directions for **F** while children finger trace each step.

Copy and Check F

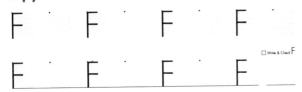

□ Write & Check F

Demonstrate **F**, saying the step-by-step directions. Children watch, then copy **F**s.
☑ Check letter: start, steps, bump

Tips

- It's fine if the small lines go all the way across the Slate or Gray Block. However, as children mature, they'll make them shorter.
- Point out that with the starting line on the left edge of the Gray Block (or Slate), the next part of the letter must be written to the right in the Gray Block. This prevents reversals.
- ☑ This is the first page in the workbook where we do ☑ Check letter. Teach the concept and components thoroughly. See page 76 of this guide for more information.
- Children may color the fish and add water or other fish.

Teach

E

| BIG LINE | I | + LITTLE LINE | Γ | + LITTLE LINE | F | + LITTLE LINE | E |

Get Started Say, "Turn to page 10. This is capital **E**. Watch me write capital **E**. I make it like this (demonstrate). Let's read this word: **EAGLE**."

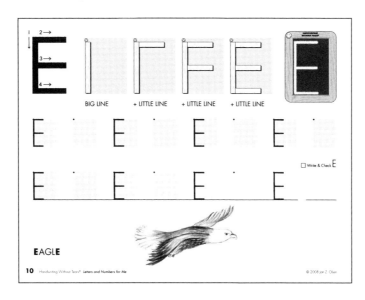

Multisensory Activities

Door Tracing
Prepare your door with the smiley face in the upper left corner. Have children reach for the top and arm trace **E**. See page 50 of this guide.

Wood Pieces
See pages 42 of this guide.

Wet–Dry–Try
See page 46 of this guide.

Finger Trace Models Step-by-Step

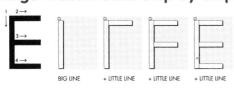

| BIG LINE | + LITTLE LINE | + LITTLE LINE | + LITTLE LINE |

Say the step-by-step directions for **E** while children finger trace each step.

Copy and Check E

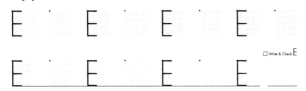

Demonstrate **E**, saying the step-by-step directions. Children watch, then copy **E**s.
☑ Check letter: start, steps, bump

Tip
- Be sure that children understand top, middle, bottom positions. Practice with a vertical big line, changing where it's held. See page 37 of this guide.
- Remember that left-handed students can write cross strokes from right to left, pulling into their hand.
- Children may color the eagle and add clouds or trees.

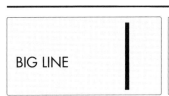
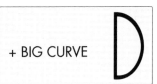

D | BIG LINE | + BIG CURVE | D

Get Started   Say, "Turn to page 11. This is capital **D**. Watch me write capital **D**. I make it like this (demonstrate). Let's read this word: **DOG**."

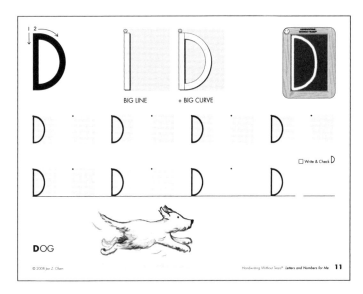

Multisensory Activities

Music and Movement
Use the *Rock, Rap, Tap & Learn* CD, *Frog Jump Letters*, Track 12. While standing, finger trace Frog Jump Capitals in the air. Let children jump between the letters.

Wood Pieces
See page 42 of this guide.

Wet–Dry–Try
See page 46 of this guide.

Finger Trace Models Step-by-Step

BIG LINE   + BIG CURVE

Say the step-by-step directions for **D** while children finger trace each step.

Copy and Check D

D   D   D   D

☐ Write & Check D

D   D   D   D

Demonstrate **D**, saying the step-by-step directions. Children watch, then copy **D**s.
☑ Check letter: start, steps, bump

Tips

- Don't worry if **D** is a little fat or skinny if it's made correctly. The shape will become more regular with practice.
- If a child is reversing **D**, play the Mystery Letter game on the Slate or on Gray Blocks. See page 56 of this guide.
- Encourage students to say the step-by-step directions for **D** out loud with you. (Start in the starting corner, big line down, frog jump back to the starting corner "ribbit," big curve.) Children get a kick out of saying "ribbit" to frog jump back to the starting corner.

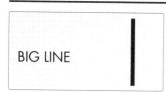 BIG LINE  + LITTLE CURVE

Get Started Say, "Turn to page 12. This is capital **P**. Watch me write capital **P**. I make it like this (demonstrate). Let's read these words: **PEAR** and **PIG**."

BIG LINE   + LITTLE CURVE

☐ Write & Check P

PEAR   **P**IG

12 Handwriting Without Tears® *Letters and Numbers for Me*   © 2008 Jan Z. Olsen

Multisensory Activities

Imaginary Writing
Follow the ball and Air Write **P**. See page 53 of this guide.

Wood Pieces
See page 42 of this guide.

Wet–Dry–Try
See page 46 of this guide.

Finger Trace Models Step-by-Step

BIG LINE   + LITTLE CURVE

Say the step-by-step directions for **P** while children finger trace each step.

Copy and Check P

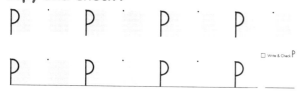

 ☐ Write & Check P

Demonstrate **P**, saying the step-by-step directions. Children watch, then copy **P**s.
☑ Check letter: start, steps, bump

Tips

- Avoid confusion with **D** and **P**. Help children make the **P** with a little curve that aims for the middle.
- Point out that with the starting line on the left edge of the Gray Block (or Slate), the next part of the letter must be written to the right in the Gray Block. This prevents reversals.
- Color the pear and the pig.

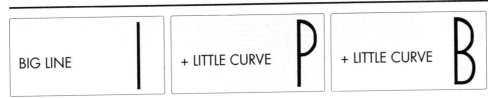

B | BIG LINE | I | + LITTLE CURVE | P | + LITTLE CURVE | B

Get Started Say, "Turn to page 13. This is capital **B**. Watch me write capital **B**. I make it like this (demonstrate). Let's read this word: **BALLOON**."

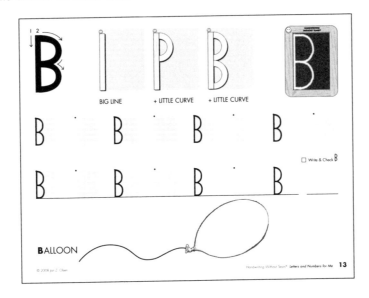

Multisensory Activities

12

Music and Movement
Use the *Rock, Rap, Tap & Learn* CD, *Frog Jump Letters*, Track 12. While standing, finger trace Frog Jump Capitals in the air. Let children jump between the letters.

Wood Pieces
See page 42 of this guide.

Wet–Dry–Try
See page 46 of this guide.

Finger Trace Models Step-by-Step

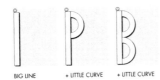

Say the step-by-step directions for **B** while children finger trace each step.

Copy and Check B

B   B   B   B

☐ Write & Check B

B   B   B   B

Demonstrate **B**, saying the step-by-step directions. Children watch, then copy **B**s.
☑ Check letter: start, steps, bump

Tips
- Re-teach top, middle, bottom positions. Practice with a vertical big line, changing where it's held. See page 37 of this guide.
- Do not be concerned if the two curves are not the same size. They'll even out with time.
- If a child is reversing **B**, play the Mystery Letter game on the Slate or on Gray Blocks. See page 56 of this guide.

Teach

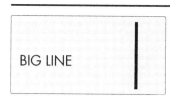 BIG LINE 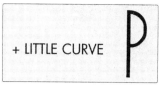 + LITTLE CURVE 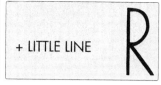 + LITTLE LINE R

Get Started Say, "Turn to page 14. This is capital **R**. Watch me write capital **R**. I make it like this (demonstrate). Let's read this word: **RAINBOW**."

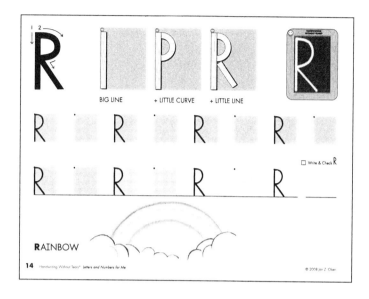

Multisensory Activities

Door Tracing
Prepare your door with the smiley face in the upper left corner. Have children reach for the top and arm trace **R**. See page 50 of this guide.

 **Wood Pieces**
See page 42 of this guide.

 **Wet–Dry–Try**
See page 46 of this guide.

Finger Trace Models Step-by-Step

BIG LINE + LITTLE CURVE + LITTLE LINE

Say the step-by-step directions for **R** while children finger trace each step.

Copy and Check R

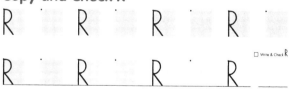

Demonstrate **R**, saying the step-by-step directions. Children watch, then copy **R**s.
☑ Check letter: start, steps, bump

Tips

- This style **R** uses just two strokes. Gently discourage children who lift their pencils from making the final little line. Encourage them to make the little curve and little line without lifting their pencils.
- Color the rainbow and add more clouds or an airplane.

 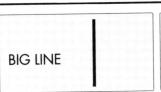  

Get Started Say, "Turn to page 15. This is capital **N**. Watch me write capital **N**. I make it like this (demonstrate). Let's read this word: **NET**."

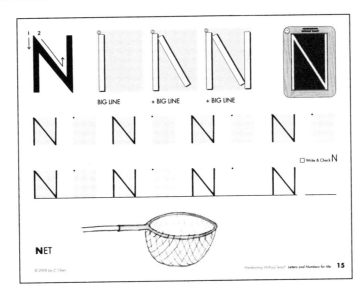

Multisensory Activities

Music and Movement

Use the *Rock, Rap, Tap & Learn* CD, *Frog Jump Letters*, Track 12. While standing, finger trace Frog Jump Capitals in the air. Let children jump between the letters.

 Wood Pieces See page 42 of this guide.

 Wet–Dry–Try See page 46 of this guide.

Finger Trace Models Step-by-Step

Say the step-by-step directions for **N** while children finger trace each step.

Copy and Check N

Demonstrate **N**, saying the step-by-step directions. Children watch, then copy **N**s.
☑ Check letter: start, steps, bump

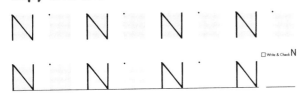

Tips

- Typically, children form this letter incorrectly, by starting at the bottom. Teach them to start at the top, in the starting corner.
- Children tend to make the diagonal stroke incorrectly, starting at the bottom of the first line. To prevent this, play the Mystery Letter game on the Slate or on Gray Blocks to make sure they frog jump back to the starting corner. See page 56 of this guide.

 | BIG LINE  | + BIG LINE  | + BIG LINE

Get Started Say, "Turn to page 16. This is capital **M**. Watch me write capital **M**. I make it like this (demonstrate). Let's read this word: **MICE**."

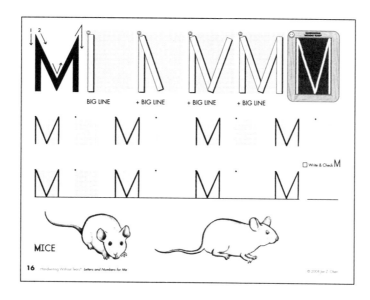

Multisensory Activities

Imaginary Writing
Use *My Teacher Writes* to demonstrate **M**. Children follow along in the air. See page 52 of this guide.

Wood Pieces
See page 42 of this guide.

Wet–Dry–Try
See page 46 of this guide.

Finger Trace Models Step-by-Step

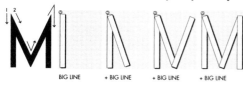

Say the step-by-step directions for **M** while children finger trace each step.

Copy and Check M

Demonstrate **M**, saying the step-by-step directions. Children watch, then copy **M**s.
☑ Check letter: start, steps, bump

Tips

- Some children find it helpful to think of making a **V** after the first big line.
- The Gray Blocks help children keep the last big line vertical.
- ☑ Check letter. Review the concept and components (start, steps, bump) of checking the letters students write. See page 76 of this guide.
- Color the mice and add cheese.

Get Started   Say, "Turn to page 17. These are all the Frog Jump Capitals. We are going to write Frog Jump Capitals and play the Mystery Letter game."

Multisensory Activities

Door Tracing
Prepare your door with the smiley face in the upper left corner. Have children reach for the top and arm trace **E**. See page 50 of this guide.

Mystery Letter on the Slate
Play the Mystery Letter game on the Slate. See page 56 of this guide.

Teach Letters Step-by-Step

Say   Here are all the Frog Jump Capitals on one page. Get ready to copy **F**. Put your pencil on the dot. Now make...

F	Big Line down, frog jump!	Little line across top, little line across middle
E	Big Line down, frog jump!	Little line across top, middle, bottom
D	Big Line down, frog jump!	Big curve to bottom corner
P	Big Line down, frog jump!	Little curve to middle
B	Big Line down, frog jump!	Little curve to middle, little curve to bottom
R	Big Line down, frog jump!	Little curve to middle, little line slides to bottom
N	Big Line down, frog jump!	Big lines slide down, big line goes up
M	Big Line down, frog jump!	Big lines slide down, up, and down

Play the Mystery Letter Game
Say   Now let's play the Mystery Letter game with Frog Jump Capitals.
Put your pencil on the dot.
Make a big line down.
Frog jump back to the top. Wait.
Make a ___. Choose a letter: **F E D P B R N M**.

Tips
* Encourage students to say the directions out loud. Children like to say "ribbit" for the frog jump.
* Notice that when the starting line is on the left edge of the Slate or Gray Block, the next part of the letter will always be on the right side. No reversals!

H	BIG LINE	+ BIG LINE	+ LITTLE LINE

Get Started   Say, "Turn to page 18. This is capital **H**. Watch me write capital **H**. I make it like this (demonstrate). Let's read this word: **HORSE**."

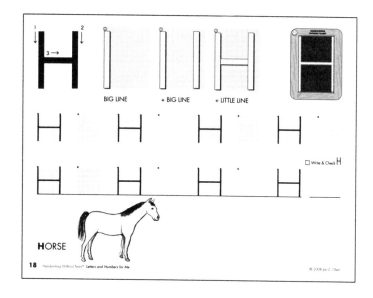

Multisensory Activities

Music and Movement
Use the *Rock, Rap, Tap & Learn* CD, *Give it a Middle*, Track 13. While standing, finger trace **H** in the air.

Wood Pieces
See page 42 of this guide.

Wet–Dry–Try
See page 46 of this guide.

Finger Trace Models Step-by-Step

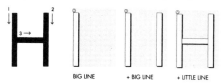

BIG LINE   + BIG LINE   + LITTLE LINE

Say the step-by-step directions for **H** while children finger trace each step.

Copy and Check H

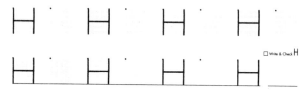

Demonstrate **H**, saying the step-by-step directions. Children watch, then copy **H**s.
☑ Check letter: start, steps, bump

Tips

- This is one of the easier letters, and it will be used for many sentences that begin: He...
- Teach that **H** does not frog jump back to the starting corner.
- Remember left-handed students can write cross strokes from right-to-left pulling into their hand.
- Color the horse and add other farm animals.

Teach

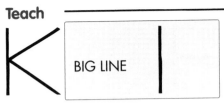  

| BIG LINE | + LITTLE LINE | + LITTLE LINE |

Get Started   Say, "Turn to page 19. This is capital **K**. Watch me write capital **K**. I make it like this (demonstrate). Let's read this word: **KOALA**."

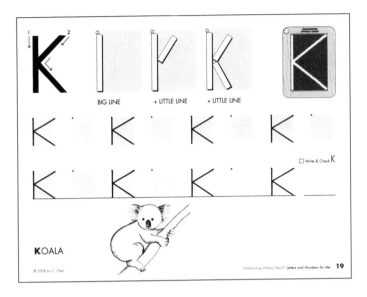

KOALA

Multisensory Activities

Music and Movement
Use the *Rock, Rap, Tap & Learn* CD, *Diagonals*, Track 5. While standing, finger trace diagonal strokes in the air.

Wood Pieces
See page 42 of this guide.

Wet–Dry–Try
See page 46 of this guide.

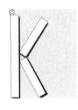

Finger Trace Models Step-by-Step

| BIG LINE | + LITTLE LINE | + LITTLE LINE |

Say the step-by-step directions for **K** while children finger trace each step.

Copy and Check K

Demonstrate **K**, saying the step-by-step directions. Children watch, then copy **K**s.
☑ Check letter: start, steps, bump

Tips

- This style **K** uses just two strokes—the big line down and then "kick" (See letter story on page 58). Gently discourage children who lift their pencils to make the final little line. Encourage them to make the little lines without lifting.
- Point out that with the starting line on the left edge of the Gray Block (or Slate), the next part of the letter must be written to the right in the Gray Block. This prevents reversals.
- Color the koala and add some bamboo.

L | BIG LINE | + LITTLE LINE | L

Get Started   Say, "Turn to page 20. This is capital **L**. Watch me write capital **L**. I make it like this (demonstrate). Let's read these words: **LAMP** and **LEAF**."

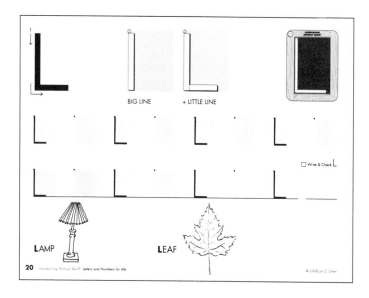

Multisensory Activities

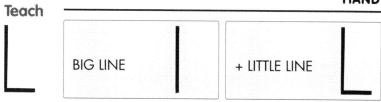

Imaginary Writing
Use Follow the Ball to demonstrate **L**. Children follow along in the air. See page 53 of this guide.

Wood Pieces
See page 42 of this guide.

Wet–Dry–Try
See page 46 of this guide.

Finger Trace Models Step-by-Step

BIG LINE | + LITTLE LINE

Say the step-by-step directions for **L** while children finger trace each step.

Copy and Check L

☐ Write & Check L

Demonstrate **L**, saying the step-by-step directions. Children watch, then copy **L**s.
☑ Check letter: start, steps, bump

Tips

• Help children really stop at the bottom before then write the little line across. This helps them keep a sharp corner.
• **L** uses just one stroke, so encourage children to keep their pencils on the page as they hit the corner and begin to write the little line.

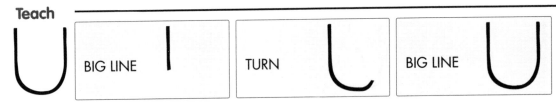

U | BIG LINE | I | TURN | U | BIG LINE | U

Get Started Say, "Turn to page 21. This is capital **U**. Watch me write capital **U**. I make it like this (demonstrate). Let's read this word: **UMBRELLA**."

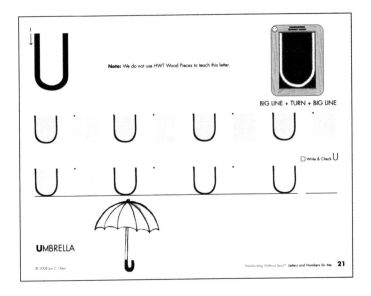

Multisensory Activities

Music and Movement
Use the *Rock, Rap, Tap & Learn* CD, *Vowels*, Track 11. While standing, finger trace diagonal strokes in the air.

Wet–Dry–Try
See page 46 of this guide.

Finger Trace Models Step-by-Step

U

Note: We do not use HWT Wood Pieces to teach this letter.

Say the step-by-step directions for **U** while children finger trace each step.

Copy and Check U

U   U   U   U

☐ Write & Check U

U   U   U   U

Demonstrate **U**, saying the step-by-step directions. Children watch, then copy **U**s.
☑ Check letter: start, steps, bump

Tips

- We do not recommend making **U** with Wood Pieces because it ends up an odd shape and size.
- Feel free to make up your own sayings. Example: For **U**, you could say: **U** go down, **U** walk on the bottom, and **U** go up.
- Color the umbrella and add some rain.

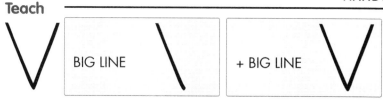

| V | BIG LINE | + BIG LINE | V |

Get Started   Say, "Turn to page 22. This is capital **V**. Watch me write capital **V**. I make it like this (demonstrate). Let's read this word: **VAN**."

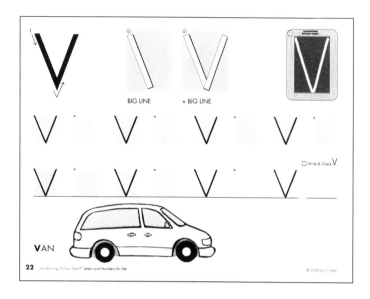

Multisensory Activities

Music and Movement
Use the *Rock, Rap, Tap & Learn* CD, *Sliding Down to the End of the Alphabet*, Track 15. Stand up and slide down to the alphabet for letters **V W X Y Z**.

Wood Pieces
See page 42 of this guide.

Wet–Dry–Try
See page 46 of this guide.

Finger Trace Models Step-by-Step

BIG LINE   + BIG LINE

Say the step-by-step directions for **V** while children finger trace each step.

Copy and Check V

V   V   V   V

☐ Write & Check V

V   V   V   V

Demonstrate **V**, saying the step-by-step directions. Children watch, then copy **V**s.
☑ Check letter: start, steps, bump

Tips

• **V** needs to have a very sharp point or else people will think it is a **U**. Tell students to make **V** sharp like a knife.

☑ Check letter. Review the concept and components (start, steps, bump) of checking the letters they write. See page 76 of this guide.

• Color the van and draw children and a driver.

Teach

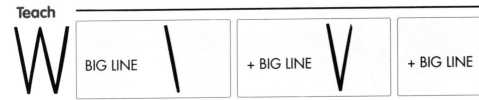  

| BIG LINE | \ | + BIG LINE | V | + BIG LINE | W | + BIG LINE | W |

Get Started   Say, "Turn to page 23. This is capital **W**. Watch me write capital **W**. I make it like this (demonstrate). Let's read this word: **WHALE**."

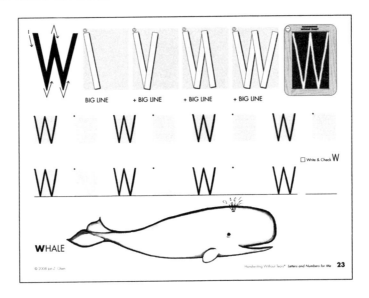

WHALE

Multisensory Activities

Door Tracing
Prepare your door with the smiley face in the upper left corner. Have children reach for the top and arm trace **W**. See page 50 of this guide.

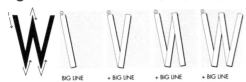

Wood Pieces
See page 42 of this guide.

Wet–Dry–Try
See page 46 of this guide.

Finger Trace Models Step-by-Step

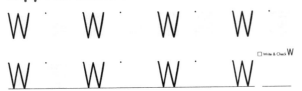

| BIG LINE | + BIG LINE | + BIG LINE | + BIG LINE |

Say the step-by-step directions for **W** while children finger trace each step.

Copy and Check W

W   W   W   W

☐ Write & Check W

W   W   W   W

Demonstrate **W**, saying the step-by-step directions. Children watch, then copy **W**s.
☑ Check letter: start, steps, bump

Tips
- Have children make a **W** by making peace signs with both hands and then putting them together.
- Tell them that **W** needs two sharp points.
- Color the whale and add water.

Teach

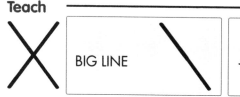

BIG LINE	+ BIG LINE

Get Started   Say, "Turn to page 24. This is capital **X**. Watch me write capital **X**. I make it like this (demonstrate). Let's read this word: **X-RAYS**."

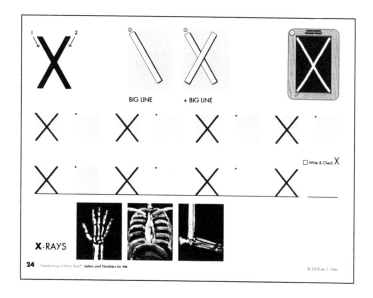

Multisensory Activities

Music and Movement
Use the *Rock, Rap, Tap & Learn* CD, *Diagonals*, Track 5. While standing, finger trace diagonal strokes in the air.

Wood Pieces
See page 42 of this guide.

Wet–Dry–Try
See page 46 of this guide.

Finger Trace Models Step-by-Step

BIG LINE   + BIG LINE

Say the step-by-step directions for **X** while children finger trace each step.

Copy and Check X

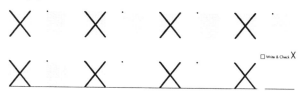

Demonstrate **X**, saying the step-by-step directions. Children watch, then copy **X**s.
☑ Check letter: start, steps, bump

Tips

- Have children make **X**s by crossing their fingers, then hands, and then arms. This is a great physical group activity. Just call out – Fingers, Hands, Arms and watch the children make bigger and bigger **X**s. And a really big one – Body, with arms and legs spread.

Teach

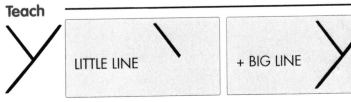

Y LITTLE LINE + BIG LINE

Get Started   Say, "Turn to page 25. This is capital **Y**. Watch me write capital **Y**. I make it like this (demonstrate). Let's read this word: **YARN**."

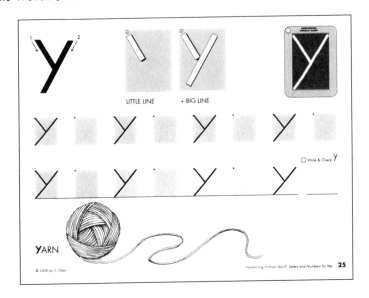

Multisensory Activities

Imaginary Writing
Use Air Writing to demonstrate **Y**. Children follow along in the air. See page 52 of this guide.

Wood Pieces
See page 42 of this guide.

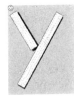

Wet–Dry–Try
See page 46 of this guide.

Finger Trace Models Step-by-Step

LITTLE LINE   + BIG LINE

Say the step-by-step directions for **Y** while children finger trace each step.

Copy and Check Y

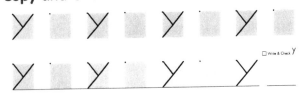

Demonstrate **Y**, saying the step-by-step directions. Children watch, then copy **Y**s.
☑ Check letter: start, steps, bump

Tips

- With this letter, it is difficult to make the first line the right length. Tell students to try to stop right in the center of the Gray Block. The second part of **Y** is a little hard to hit exactly right (corner – end of first stroke – corner) so don't worry too much about it.
- You and your students may also choose to write the **Y** that looks like this **Y** – a little **v** with a little line.
- Color the yarn.

Teach

| LITTLE LINE | + BIG LINE | + LITTLE LINE |

Get Started   Say, "Turn to page 26. This is capital **Z**. Watch me write capital **Z**. I make it like this (demonstrate). Let's read this word: **ZEBRA**."

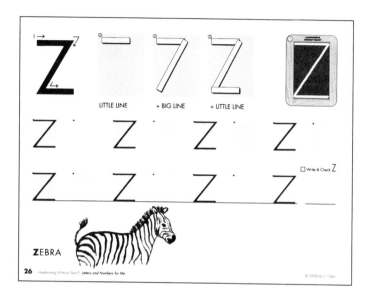

Multisensory Activities

Music and Movement
Use the *Rock, Rap, Tap & Learn* CD. *Sliding Down to the End of the Alphabet*, Track 15. Stand up and slide down to the alphabet for letters **V W X Y Z**.

 **Wood Pieces**
See page 42 of this guide.

 Wet–Dry–Try
See page 46 of this guide.

Finger Trace Models Step-by-Step

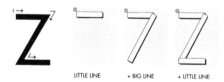

| LITTLE LINE | + BIG LINE | + LITTLE LINE |

Say the step-by-step directions for **Z** while children finger trace each step.

Copy and Check Z

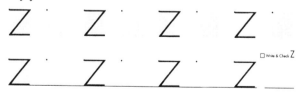

Demonstrate **Z**, saying the step-by-step directions. Children watch, then copy **Z**s.
☑ Check letter: start, steps, bump

Tips

- This is a really fun letter. Just get the children started in the starting corner and then it is zoom across, zoom down to the other corner, and zoom across.
- ☑ Check letter. Review the concept and components (start, steps, bump) of checking the letters students write. See page 76 of this guide.

Activity Page – WORDS FOR ME

Children get lots of exposure to capital letters in their daily lives. Here are some words that children see in buildings and out on the street.

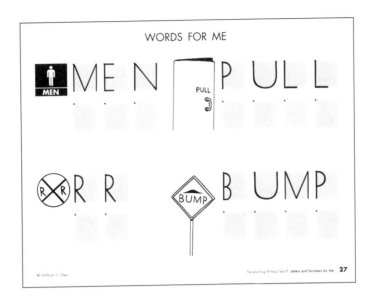

Tell them...

Look at these pictures. Two are building signs and two are road signs. **MEN** tells us that the restroom is for men or boys. **PULL** tells us to pull to open the door. **RR** stands for railroad and the **X** stands for crossing. **BUMP** tells us that the road has a bump and that the driver should slow down.

How do I teach this?

Give verbal directions for each word and letter.

Say   Find the word MEN. Find the letter **M**. Get ready to copy **M** in the Gray Block.
Put your pencil on the dot.

M	Big line down, frog jump! Big lines slide down, up, and down.
E	Big line down, frog jump! Little line across top, middle, bottom.
N	Big line down, frog jump! Big line slides to bottom, big line goes up.

Say   Find the word **PULL**. Find the letter **P**. Get ready to copy **P** in the Gray Block.
Put your pencil on the dot.

P	Big line down, frog jump! Little curve to middle.
U	Down, turn, and up.
L	Big line down, little line across.
L	Big line down, little line across.

Say   Find the railroad sign. Find the letters **RR**. Get ready to copy **R** in the Gray Block.
Put your pencil on the dot.

R	Big line down, frog jump! Little curve to middle, little lines slides down.
R	Big line down, frog jump! Little curve to middle, little lines slides down.

Say   Find the **BUMP** sign. Find the word **BUMP**. Get ready to copy **B** in the Gray Block.
Put your pencil on the dot.

B	Big line down, frog jump! Little curve to middle, little curve to bottom.
U	Down, turn, and up.
M	Big line down, frog jump! Big lines slide down, up, and down.
P	Big line down, frog jump! Little curve to middle.

BIG CURVE

Get Started Say, "Turn to page 28. This is capital **C**. Watch me write capital **C**. I make it like this (demonstrate). Let's read this word: **CAR**."

Multisensory Activities

Door Tracing
Prepare your door with the smiley face in the upper left corner. Have children reach for the top and arm trace **C**. See page 50 of this guide.

Wood Pieces
See page 42 of this guide.

Wet–Dry–Try
See page 46 of this guide.

Finger Trace Models Step-by-Step

BIG CURVE

Say the step-by-step directions for **C** while children finger trace each step.

Copy and Check C

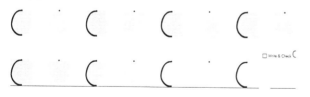

Demonstrate **C**, saying the step-by-step directions. Children watch, then copy **C**s.
☑ Check letter: start, steps, bump

Tips
- Tell students that this is the first capital that doesn't start in the starting corner. **C** still starts at the top but in the center not the corner.
- To help children remember which way to go, get the Slate out and tell them to start **C** by going over to say "hello" to the smiley face.
- Color the car and add a driver or another car.

Teach

  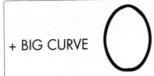

BIG CURVE

+ BIG CURVE

Get Started Say, "Turn to page 29. This is capital **O**. Watch me write capital **O**. I make it like this (demonstrate). Let's read these words: **ORANGE** and **OCTOPUS**."

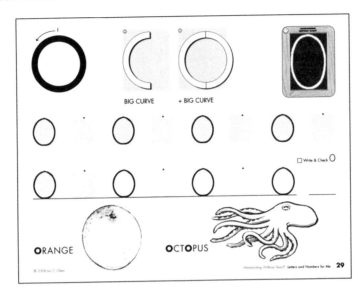

Multisensory Activities

Laser Letters
Use a laser and trace **O** on the board or on an easel. Children follow along in the air. See page 53 of this guide.

Wood Pieces
See page 42 of this guide.

Wet–Dry–Try
See page 46 of this guide.

Finger Trace Models Step-by-Step

BIG CURVE   + BIG CURVE

Say the step-by-step directions for **O** while children finger trace each step.

Copy and Check O

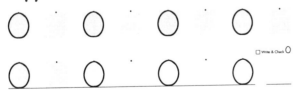

☐ Write & Check O

Demonstrate **O**, saying the step-by-step directions. Children watch, then copy **O**s.
☑ Check letter: start, steps, bump

Tips

- Explain that **O** is the only letter that when you say it, your mouth makes the shape of the letter you are saying. Have the students make **O** mouth shapes.
- Be sure to teach that we make a **C** to start a circle and a **C** to start an **O**.
- Tell students that they write zero the exact same way. Then ask them what sound the last part of the number zero makes—it is **O**!

Teach

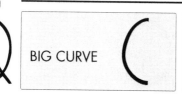  

Q BIG CURVE + BIG CURVE + LITTLE LINE

Get Started Say, "Turn to page 30. This is capital **Q**. Watch me write capital **Q**. I make it like this (demonstrate). Let's read this word: **QUILT**."

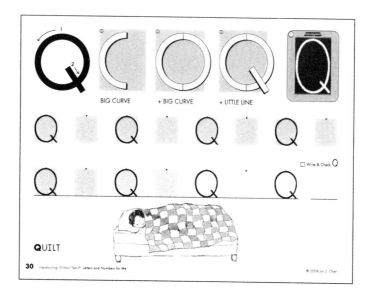

Multisensory Activities

Door Tracing
Prepare your door with the smiley face in the upper left corner. Have children reach for the top and arm trace **Q**. See page 50 of this guide.

Wood Pieces
See page 42 of this guide.

Wet–Dry–Try
See page 46 of this guide.

Finger Trace Models Step-by-Step

BIG CURVE   + BIG CURVE   + LITTLE LINE

Say the step-by-step directions for **Q** while children finger trace each step.

Copy and Check Q

Demonstrate **Q**, saying the step-by-step directions. Children watch, then copy **Q**s.
☑ Check letter: start, steps, bump

Tips

- This is just an **O** with a little tail.
- To help children remember which way to go, get the Slate out and tell them to start **C** by going over to say "hello" to the smiley face.
- Color the quilt squares.

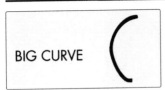

BIG CURVE

+ LITTLE LINE

+ LITTLE LINE

Get Started Say, "Turn to page 31. This is capital **G**. Watch me write capital **G**. I make it like this (demonstrate). Let's read these words: **GUMBALLS** and **GLOVES**."

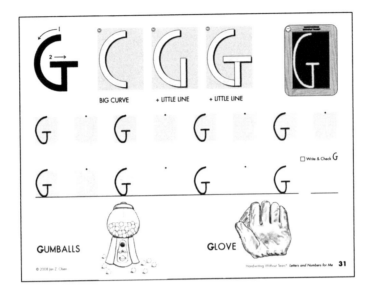

Multisensory Activities

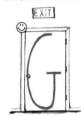

Door Tracing
Prepare your door with the smiley face in the upper left corner. Have children reach for the top and arm trace **G**. See page 50 of this guide.

Wood Pieces
See page 42 of this guide.

Wet–Dry–Try
See page 46 of this guide.

Finger Trace Models Step-by-Step

BIG CURVE   **+ LITTLE LINE**   **+ LITTLE LINE**

Say the step-by-step directions for **G** while children finger trace each step.

Copy and Check G

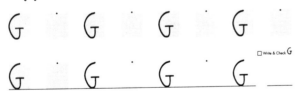

☐ Write & Check G

Demonstrate **G**, saying the step-by-step directions. Children watch, then copy **G**s.
☑ Check letter: start, steps, bump

Tips
- To reinforce the center starting and the correct formation habits for the Magic C Capitals, play the Mystery Letter game on the Slate or on Gray Blocks. See page 56 of this guide.
- ☑ Check Letter. Review the concept and components (start, steps, bump) of checking the letters they write. See page 76 of this guide.
- Color the gumballs and add a baseball to the glove.

Review Magic C Capitals C O Q G

Get Started   Say, "Turn to page 32. These are the Magic C Capitals. We are going to write Magic C Capitals and play the Mystery Game.

Multisensory Activities

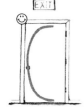

Door Tracing

Prepare your door with the smiley face in the upper left corner. Have children reach for the top center and arm trace letters. To get **C O Q G** started correctly, tell students to go over and say "hello" to the smiley face. See page 50 of this guide.

Mystery Letter on the Slate

Play the Mystery Letter game on the Slate. See page 56 of this guide.

Teach Letters Step-by-Step

Say   Here are all the Magic C Capitals on one page.

Letters **C O Q G** begin with a Magic C. Get ready to copy **C**. Put your pencil on the dot.
       Make a Magic C. Now make...

O   Make a Magic C. Keep on going around. Stop at the top.

Q   Make a Magic C. Keep on going around. Stop at the top. Add a little line.

G   Make a Magic C. Go up. Add a little line.

Play the Mystery Game

Say   Now let's play the Mystery Letter game for Magic C Capitals.
Put your pencil on the dot.
Make a Magic C.
Turn Magic C into ___ (**O Q G** or leave as **C**).

Tip

- One side of the Slate has the words Handwriting Without Tears® at the top center. Use this side to help children find the center.

 LITTLE CURVE

 + LITTLE CURVE

Get Started Say, "Turn to page 33. This is capital **S**. Watch me write capital **S**. I make it like this (demonstrate). Let's read this word: **SAW**."

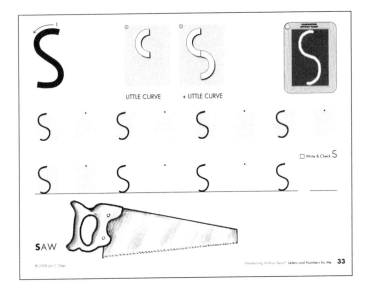

Multisensory Activities

Imaginary Writing
Use My Teacher Writes to demonstrate **S**. Children follow along in the air. See page 52 of this guide.

Wood Pieces
See page 42 of this guide.

Wet–Dry–Try
See page 46 of this guide.

Finger Trace Models Step-by-Step

LITTLE CURVE   + LITTLE CURVE

Say the step-by-step directions for **S** while children finger trace each step.

Copy and Check S

S   S   S   S

☐ Write & Check S

S   S   S   S

Demonstrate **S**, saying the step-by-step directions. Children watch, then copy **S**s.
☑ Check letter: start, steps, bump

Tips
- Teach children to start **S** with a Magic c and then "stop, drop, and roll."
- To help children remember which way to start, use the Slate and tell them to start **S** by going to say "hello" to the smiley face.
- Color the saw and draw a seesaw.

Teach

 BIG LINE

 + BIG LINE

 + LITTLE LINE

Get Started Say, "Turn to page 34. This is capital **A**. Watch me write capital **A**. I make it like this (demonstrate). Let's read this word: **ALLIGATOR**."

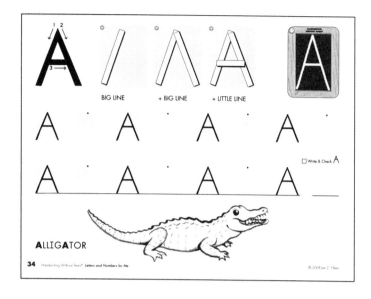

Multisensory Activities

Music and Movement
Use the *Rock, Rap, Tap & Learn* CD, *Give it a Middle*, Track 13. While standing, finger trace **A** in the air.

Wood Pieces
See page 42 of this guide.

Wet–Dry–Try
See page 46 of this guide.

Finger Trace Models Step-by-Step

BIG LINE   + BIG LINE   + LITTLE LINE

Say the step-by-step directions for **A** while children finger trace each step.

Copy and Check A

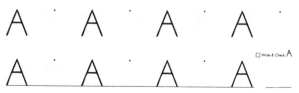

Demonstrate **A**, saying the step-by-step directions. Children watch, then copy **A**s.
☑ Check letter: start, steps, bump

Tips
- Pay attention to this one! Children often start **A** from the bottom, so be sure to teach them to start at the top, in the top center.
- Remember that left-handed students can write cross strokes from right-to-left, pulling into their hand.

Teach

| BIG LINE | + LITTLE LINE | + LITTLE LINE |

Get Started Say, "Turn to page 35. This is capital **I**. Watch me write capital **I**. I make it like this (demonstrate). Let's read this word: **IGLOOS**."

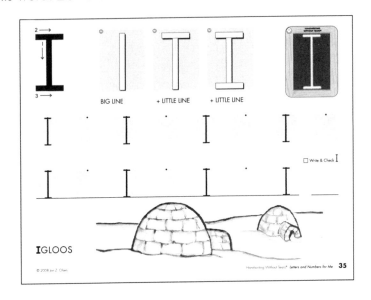

Multisensory Activities

Music and Movement
Use the *Rock, Rap, Tap & Learn* CD, *Give it a Top*, Track 14. Finger trace **I** in the air.

Wood Pieces
See page 42 of this guide.

Wet–Dry–Try
See page 46 of this guide.

Finger Trace Models Step-by-Step

BIG LINE   + LITTLE LINE   + LITTLE LINE

Say the step-by-step directions for **I** while children finger trace each step.

Copy and Check I

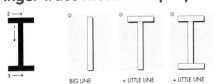

Demonstrate **I**, saying the step-by-step directions. Children watch, then copy **I**s.
☑ Check letter: start, steps, bump

Tips

- It is better to teach **I** with a top and bottom so children recognize it as being different from the number **1** and lowercase **l**.
- Remember that left-handed students can write cross strokes from right to left, pulling into their hand.
- Color the igloos and add a polar bear.

BIG LINE	+ LITTLE LINE

Get Started Say, "Turn to page 36. This is capital **T**. Watch me write capital **T**. I make it like this (demonstrate). Let's read this word: **TURTLE**."

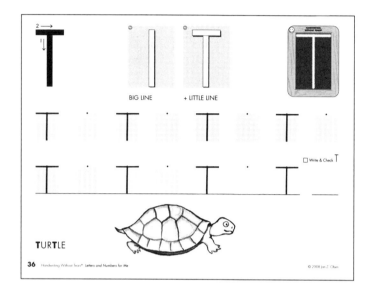

BIG LINE + LITTLE LINE

☐ Write & Check T

TURTLE

36 Handwriting Without Tears® *Letters and Numbers for Me* © 2008 Jan Z. Olsen

Multisensory Activities

Door Tracing
Prepare your door with the smiley face in the upper left corner. Have children reach for the top and arm trace **T**. See page 50 of this guide.

Wood Pieces
See page 42 of this guide.

Wet–Dry–Try
See page 46 of this guide.

Finger Trace Models Step-by-Step

BIG LINE + LITTLE LINE

Say the step-by-step directions for **T** while children finger trace each step.

Copy and Check T

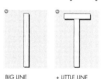

☐ Write & Check T

Demonstrate **T**, saying the step-by-step directions. Children watch, then copy **T**s.
☑ Check letter: start, steps, bump

Tips

- Tell the students that **T** is for top and to start at the top and cross at the top.
- ☑ Check letter. Review the concept and components (start, steps, bump) of checking the letters students write. See page 76 of this guide.

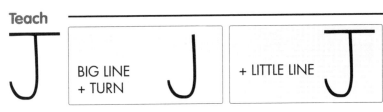

J

| BIG LINE + TURN | + LITTLE LINE |

Get Started   Say, "Turn to page 37. This is capital **J**. Watch me write capital **J**. I make it like this (demonstrate). Let's read these words: **JUICE** and **JEANS**."

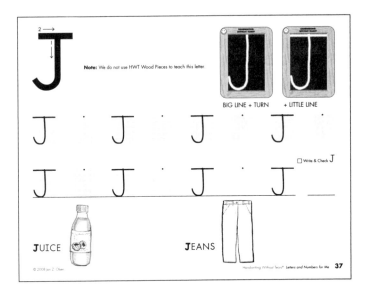

Multisensory Activities

Music and Movement
Use the *Rock, Rap, Tap & Learn* CD, *Give it a Top*, Track 14. Finger trace **J** in the air.

Wet–Dry–Try
See page 46 of this guide.

Finger Trace Models Step-by-Step

Say the step-by-step directions for **J** while children finger trace each step.

Copy and Check J

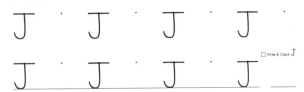

Demonstrate **J**, saying the step-by-step directions. Children watch, then copy **J**s.
☑ Check letter: start, steps, bump

Tips
• We do not recommend making **J** with Wood Pieces because it ends up being an odd shape and size.
• Remember that left-handed students can write cross strokes from right to left, pulling into their hand.
• Color the juice and jeans.

Activity Page – WORDS FOR ME, CAPITAL LETTERS FOR ME

Capital letters are the first letters children notice. Capital letters appear on important signs that children see every day. This page will help them read and write capitals.

Words for Me

Tell them...

Look at these pictures. I will say a word. You point to the picture that goes with the word: **STOP**, **WALK**, **GIRLS**, **BUS**. Have you seen these words before? Where did you see them?

How do I teach this?

Give verbal directions for each word and letter.

Say   Find the word **STOP**. Find the letter **S**. Get ready to copy **S** in the Gray Block.
        Put your pencil on the dot...

S	Make a little curve (little Magic c). Turn. Make another little curve.
T	Make a big line down, little line across top.
O	Make a Magic C. Keep on going around. Stop at the top.
P	Big line down, frog jump! Little curve to middle.

Follow this pattern for words **WALK**, **GIRLS**, **BUS**.

Capital Letters for Me

Tell them...

Here are all the capital letters in the alphabet. They are in ABC or alphabetical order.

How do I teach this?

Have children sing the alphabet and point to each letter as they sing.
Give verbal directions for each letter.

Say   Find capital **A**. Get ready to copy **A** in the Gray Block.
        Put your pencil on the dot...

A	Big line slides down, jump to the dot. Big line slides down, little line across.
B	Big line down, frog jump to the dot. Little curve to middle, little curve to bottom.

For a list of detailed verbal directions for all capital letters, visit **www.hwtears.com/click**.

LOWERCASE

Teach

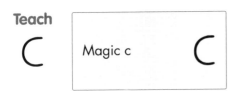

Magic c

Get Started   Say, "Turn to page 40. This is lowercase **c**. Watch me write lowercase **c**. I make it like this. (Say step-by-step directions as you demonstrate.) Let's read this sentence: **C is for cow.**"

Magic c

☐ Write & Check C

C is for **c**ow.

Multisensory Activities

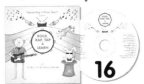

16

Music and Movement
Use the *Rock, Rap, Tap & Learn* CD, *CAPITALS and lowercase*, Track 16. Have children sing and copy as you model capital **C** and lowercase **c** on the board. Combine this song with Letter Size and Place when the lyrics say, "A capital **C** is tall, tall, tall, A lowercase **c** is small, small, small)."

C   c

Letter Size and Place
Demonstrate capital **C** and lowercase **c**. Hold up hand with the capital first. See page 54 of this guide.

Finger Trace Models Step-by-Step

Magic c

Say the step-by-step directions for **c** while children finger trace each step.

Copy and Check c

☐ Write & Check C

Demonstrate **c**, saying the step-by-step directions. Children watch, then copy **c**s.
☑ Check letter: start, steps, bump

Tips
- If **c** is too skinny start on the dot and then travel on the top line before curving down.
- Emphasize tall and small size.
- Teach left-handed students to copy from the model on the right.
- Children may color the cow and add grass.

 | Magic c |  keep on going | stop | ◯

Get Started   Say, "Turn to page 41. This is lowercase **o**. Watch me write lowercase **o**. I make it like this. (Say step-by-step directions as you demonstrate.) Let's read this sentence: **O is for octopus.**"

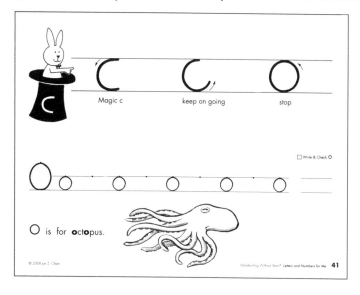

Multisensory Activities

Wet–Dry–Try
Use the Blackboard with Double Lines. See page 48 of this guide.

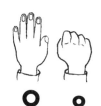

Letter Size and Place
Demonstrate **O** and lowercase **o**. Hold up the left hand representing the capital first. See page 54 of this guide.

Finger Trace Models Step-by-Step

Say the step-by-step directions for **o** while children finger trace each step.

Copy and Check o

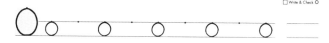

Demonstrate **o**, saying the step-by-step directions. Children watch, then copy **o**s.
☑ Check letter: start, steps, bump

Tips
- If **o** doesn't start at the top, use the Blackboard with Double Lines with Wet–Dry–Try. See page 48.
- Teach left-handed students to copy from the model on the right.
- Children may color the octopus or draw other **o** pictures such as owl or orange.

Teach

| S | little Magic c C | turn down C | curve around S |

Get Started Say, "Turn to page 42. This is lowercase **s**. Watch me write lowercase **s**. I make it like this. (Say step-by-step directions as you demonstrate.) Let's read this sentence: **S is for snowman.**"

Multisensory Activities

Letter Story
See page 59 of this guide.

S   s

Letter Size and Place
Demonstrate capital **S** and lowercase **s**. Hold up hand with the capital first. See page 54 of this guide.

Finger Trace Models Step-by-Step

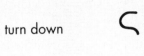

Say the step-by-step directions for **s** while children finger trace each step.

Copy and Check s

Demonstrate **s**, saying the step-by-step directions. Children watch, then copy **s**s.
☑ Check letter: start, steps, bump

Tips

- If **s** doesn't start at the top, use the Blackboard with Double Lines with Wet–Dry–Try. See page 48.
- If **s** goes the wrong way, use the Slate Chalkboard. Start at the top center and move chalk toward the ☺ with a little c stroke.
- Teach left-handed students to copy from the model on the right.
- Children may color the snowman.

© 2008 Jan Z. Olsen

Activity Page – WORDS WITH S

You know that letter **s** is tricky. Not only is **s** reversible, it changes directions during the stroke. Here's a page to give your budding writers extra practice with **s**.

Tell them...

Look at these pictures. I will say a word and you point to the picture that goes with it: **sun**...**star**...**sad**...**sit**...**sea**...**seal**. Guess what? All of these words start with letter **s**.

How do I teach this?

Talk about each picture and word. Help children spell and say the word before tracing **s**.

sun   Find the picture of the sun. Find the word **sun** under the picture. **Sun** starts with **s**.
We will spell the word **sun**: **s – u – n**. Let's say it slowly **s—un**.
Now put your pencil on the dot.
Trace **s**.

star   Find the picture of the star. Find the word **star** under the picture. **Star** starts with **s**.
We will spell the word **star**: **s – t – a – r**. Let's say it slowly **s—tar**.
Now put your pencil on the dot.
Trace **s**.

sad   Find the picture of the sad boy. Find the word **sad** under the picture. **Sad** starts with **s**.
We will spell the word **sad**: **s – a – d**. Let's say it slowly **s—ad**.
Now put your pencil on the dot.
Trace **s**.

sit   Find the picture of the boy sitting. Find the word **sit** under the picture. **Sit** starts with **s**.
We will spell the word **sit**: **s – i – t**. Let's say it slowly **s—it**.
Now put your pencil on the dot.
Trace **s**.

sea   Find the picture of the sea. Find the word **sea** under the picture. **Sea** starts with **s**.
We will spell the word **sea**: **s – e – a**. Let's say it slowly **s—ea**.
Now put your pencil on the dot.
Trace **s**.

seal   Find the picture of a seal. Find the word **seal** under the picture. **Seal** starts with **s**.
Let's spell the word **seal**: **s – e – a – l**. Let's say it slowly **s—eal**.
Now put your pencil on the dot.
Trace **s**.

V | slide down | \ | slide up | V

Get Started   Say, "Turn to page 44. This is lowercase **v**. Watch me write lowercase **v**. I make it like this (demonstrate). Let's read this sentence: **V is for violin.**"

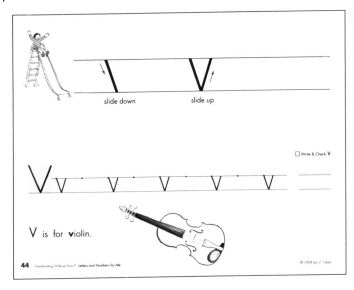

Multisensory Activities

Imaginary Writing
Use Air Writing to demonstrate **v**. Children follow along in the air. See page 52 of this guide.

Letter Size and Place
V is tall. Lowercase **v** is small. See page 54 of this guide.

Finger Trace Models Step-by-Step

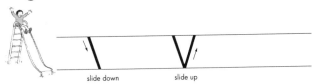

Say the step-by-step directions for **v** while children finger trace each step.

Copy and Check v

Demonstrate **v**, saying the step-by-step directions. Children watch, then copy **v**s.
☑ Check letter: start, steps, bump

Tips
- If **v** doesn't start at the top, use the Blackboard with Double Lines with Wet–Dry–Try. See page 48.
- Emphasize tall and small size.
- Emphasize bumping the bottom line.
- Teach left-handed students to copy from the model on the right.

Teach

W | slide down and up V | down and up W

Get Started   Say, "Turn to page 45. This is lowercase **w**. Watch me write lowercase **w**. I make it like this (demonstrate). Let's read this sentence: **W is for whale.**"

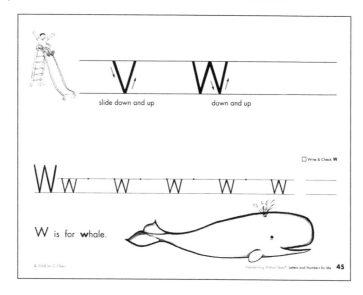

Multisensory Activities

16

Music and Movement
Use the *Rock, Rap, Tap & Learn* CD, *CAPITALS and lowercase*, Track 16. Have children sing and copy as you model capital **W** and lowercase **w** on the board. You may combine this song with Letter Size and Place when the lyrics say, "A capital **W** is tall, tall, tall, A lowercase **w** is small, small, small."

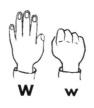

W   w

Letter Size and Place
Demonstrate capital **W** and lowercase **w**. Hold up hand with the capital first. See page 54 of this guide.

Finger Trace Models Step-by-Step

slide down and up   down and up

Say the step-by-step directions for **w** while children finger trace each step.

Copy and Check w

Ww w w w w

Demonstrate **w**, saying the step-by-step directions. Children watch, then copy **w**s.
☑ Check letter: start, steps, bump

Tips

- If the diagonal in **w** is challenging, use the Blackboard with Double Lines and Wet–Dry–Try. See page 48 of this guide.
- Emphasize bumping the bottom line.
- Teach left-handed students to copy from the model on the right.
- Check Your Teaching, page 146 of this guide.

Teach

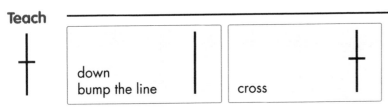

down
bump the line

cross

Get Started Say, "Turn to page 46. This is lowercase **t**. Watch me write lowercase **t**. I make it like this (demonstrate). Let's read this sentence: **T is for tow truck.**"

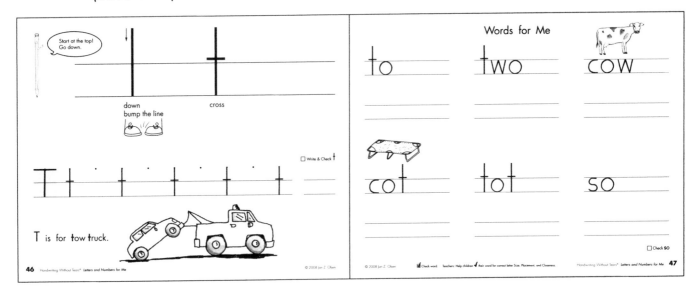

Multisensory Activities

Letter Story
See page 59 of this guide.

Finger Trace Models Step-by-Step

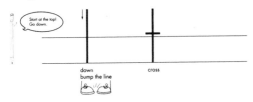

Say the step-by-step directions while tracing.
Children watch, then trace **t**.

Copy and Check t

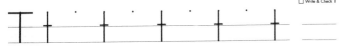

Demonstrate **t**, saying the step-by-step directions.
Children watch, then copy **t**s.
☑ Check letter: start, steps, bump

Copy and Check Words

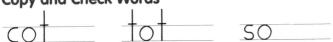

Demonstrate **so.**
Emphasize that the letters are close.
Children watch, then copy.
☑ Check letter: start, steps, bump

Tips

- This is the first page in the workbook where we do ☑ Check word. Teach the concept and components (letter size, placement, and closeness) thoroughly. See page 76 of this guide for more information.
- Students cross **t** according to their handedness.
- Mark arrows → for right-handed students. Mark arrows ← for left-handed students.

Multisensory Activity – MAGIC C BUNNY

The Magic C Bunny helps you teach **c**-based lowercase letters **a d g o q**. The Magic C Bunny puppet will bring your lessons to life.

What does the Magic C Bunny do?
- He changes letter **c** into new letters. That's the magic trick.
- He plays Mystery Letter and Voice games.
- He makes learning fun.
- He creates a good Magic c habit for **a d g o** and even **q**.

17

Multisensory Activities
Music and Movement
Have fun with the *Magic C Rap*, Track 17. This song is a great way to get your students engaged and excited about Magic c letters.
- Introduce Magic **c** while playing the *Magic C Rap*.
- Teach children to sing the chorus:

    Magic c, c for a d and g
    Magic c, c for a d and g
    Magic c, c for a d and g
    And before you're through do o and q

- Introduce the song before demonstrating Magic c letters on the board. Use the Voices activity and have Magic C Bunny whisper which voices your class should use into your ear.

Make the Magic C Bunny

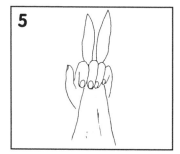

1
Open paper napkin. Hold by one corner.

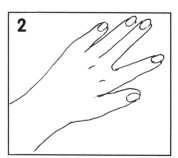

2
Spread index and middle fingers apart.

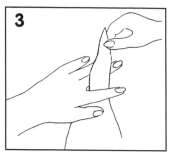

3
Pull corner between your index and middle fingers. (First ear)

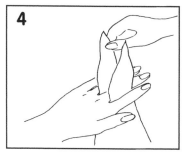

4
Take the next corner. Pull corner between your middle and ring fingers. (Second ear)

5
Fold fingers into palm.

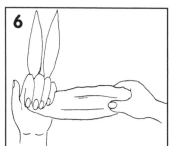

6
Pull napkin out to side.

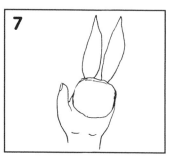

7
Wrap napkin over fingers and tuck into hand.

8
Add the face with a pen. It's a bunny! You may slip the bunny off your fingers and give it to a child. Tape or staple the napkin to hold it.

Teach

| a | Magic c | C | up like a helicopter | G | bump | a | back down bump | a |

Get Started Say, "Turn to page 48. This is lowercase **a**. Watch me write lowercase **a**. I make it like this (demonstrate). Let's read this sentence: **A is for alligator.**"

Multisensory Activities

Music and Movement
Use the *Rock, Rap, Tap & Learn* CD, *Magic C Rap*, Track 17. See page 117 of this guide.

Voices
Demonstrate **a** on the board using the Voices activity. See page 55 of this guide.

Finger Trace Models Step-by-Step

Say the step-by-step directions for **a** while children finger trace each step.

Copy and Check a

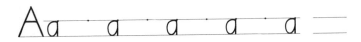

Demonstrate **a**, saying the step-by-step directions. Children watch, then copy **a**s.
☑ Check letter: start, steps, bump

Tips
- If **a** is too skinny, start on the dot and travel on the top line before curving down.
- After learning **d** and **g**, play the Mystery Letter game on the Blackboard with Double Lines, page 57.
- Children may color the alligator and add rocks, grass, water, etc.

| d | Magic c | C | up like a helicopter | G | up higher | d | back down bump | d |

Get Started   Say, "Turn to page 49. This is lowercase **d**. Watch me write lowercase **d**. I make it like this (demonstrate). Let's read this sentence: **D is for duck.**"

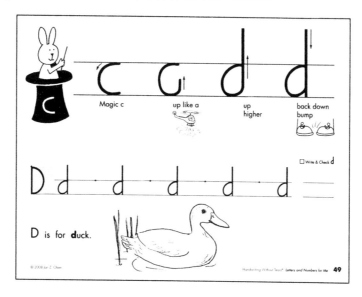

Multisensory Activities

Voices
Demonstrate **d** on the board using the Voices activity. See page 55 of this guide.

Letter Size and Place
Review **a** as a small letter and demonstrate **d** as a tall letter. See page 54 of this guide.

Finger Trace Models Step-by-Step

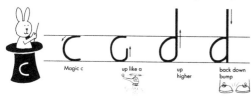

Say the step-by-step directions for **d** while children finger trace each step.

Copy and Check d

Demonstrate **d**, saying the step-by-step directions. Children watch, then copy **d**s.
☑ Check letter: start, steps, bump

Tips

- If **d** is short, go up higher like a helicopter.
- If a child doesn't retrace the line down: Tell the child to think of sliding down a pole. "Hang on until your feet touch the ground."

	Magic c	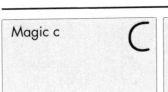	up like a helicopter bump		back down		turn	

Get Started   Say, "Turn to page 50. This is lowercase **g**. Watch me write lowercase **g**. I make it like this (demonstrate). Let's read this sentence: **G is for goat.**"

Multisensory Activities

Music and Movement
Use the *Rock, Rap, Tap & Learn* CD, Track 17. See page 117 of this guide.

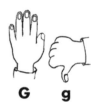

Letter Story
See page 58 of this guide.

Letter Size and Place
Demonstrate capital **G** and lowercase **g**. Hold up hand with the capital first.

Say the step-by-step directions for **g** while children finger trace each step.

Finger Trace Models Step-by-Step

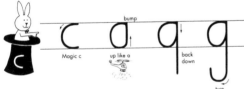

Copy and Check g

□ Write & Check g

Demonstrate **g**, saying the step-by-step directions. Children watch, then copy **g**s.
☑ Check letter: start, steps, bump

Copy and Check Sentences

Demonstrate **I saw a goat.**
Emphasize capitalization, word spacing, and period.
☑ Check sentence: capital, spaces, end

Tips

- This is the first page in the workbook where we do ☑ Check sentence. Teach the concept and components (capital, spaces, end) thoroughly. See page 76 for more information.
- If spacing is a problem when writing words, teach students to put letters in a word close to each other. Have them put their index fingers up and bring them close together without touching. Tell them, "In a word, the letters are close, but don't touch." Draw fingers for them!
- Check Your Teaching, page 146 of this guide.

Get Started   Say, "Turn to page 52. This is lowercase **u**. Watch me write lowercase **u**. I make it like this (demonstrate). Let's read this sentence: **U is for umbrella.**"

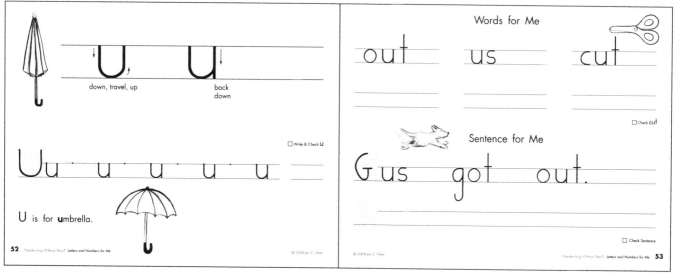

Multisensory Activities

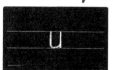

Wet–Dry–Try
Use the Blackboard with Double Lines.
See page 48 of this guide.

Imaginary Writing
Follow the Ball and air write
u. Children follow along in the
air. See page 53 of this guide.

Finger Trace Models Step-by-Step

Say the step-by-step directions for **u**
while children finger trace each step.

Copy and Check u

Demonstrate **u**, saying the step-by-step directions.
Children watch, then copy **u**.
☑ Check letter: start, steps, bump

Copy and Check Words

Demonstrate **cut**
Emphasize that the letters are close.
Children watch, then copy.
☑ Check word: size, placement, closeness

Copy and Check Words and Sentences

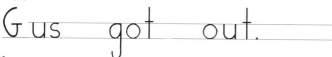

Demonstrate **Gus got out.**
Emphasize capitalization, word spacing, and period.
☑ Check sentence: capital, spaces, end

Tips

- Teach that **U** and **u** are similar except little **u** has a line.
- If **u** is too pointed like **v**, travel on the bottom line. Take at least two steps on the line and then come straight up.

 down dot

Get Started Say, "Turn to page 54. This is lowercase **i**. Watch me write lowercase **i**. I make it like this (demonstrate). Let's read this sentence: **I is for insects.**"

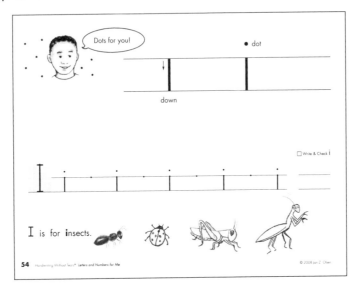

Multisensory Activities

Music and Movement
Use the *Rock, Rap, Tap & Learn* CD, *Vowels*, Track 11. Have children sing the chorus.

Wet–Dry–Try
Use the Blackboard with Double Lines. See page 48 of this guide.

Finger Trace Models Step-by-Step
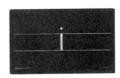

Say the step-by-step directions for **i** while children finger trace each step.

Copy and Check i

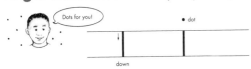

Demonstrate **i**, saying the step-by-step directions. Children watch, then copy **i**s.
☑ Check letter: start, steps, bump

Tips
- Teach the dot.
- Teach children to make the line before the dot. Be flexible about what the dots look like. Allow a little creativity.
- Teach that **I** and **i** are different and **i** is never used alone.
- Children may color the insects.

| e | start
hit the ball | — | run the bases | $\cap$ | stop | e |

Get Started Say, "Turn to page 55. This is lowercase **e**. Watch me write lowercase **e**. I make it like this (demonstrate). Let's read this sentence: **E is for elephant.**"

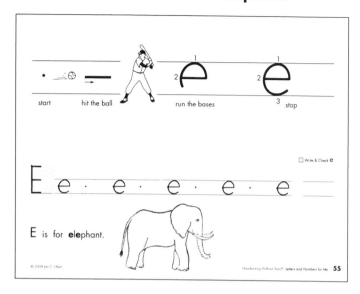

Multisensory Activities

Letter Story
See page 58 of this guide.

Wet–Dry–Try
Use the Blackboard with Double Lines. See page 48 of this guide.

Finger Trace Models Step-by-Step

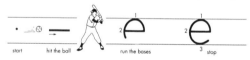

Say the step-by-step directions for **e** while children finger trace each step.

Copy and Check e

Demonstrate **e**, saying the step-by-step directions. Children watch, then copy **e**s.
☑ Check letter: start, steps, bump

Tips

- If the beginning of the line isn't straight, practice writing straight dashes between the lines.
- Lowercase **e** does not begin on a line—it begins in the air between the lines. A visual cue may be needed (a dot) for the child to become comfortable with this concept.
- Remind the child that it is not a home run, "so only run to third base!"
- Children may color the elephant and add grass and food.

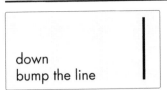

down
bump the line

Get Started Say, "Turn to page 56. This is lowercase **l**. Watch me write lowercase **l**. I make it like this (demonstrate). Let's read this sentence: **L is for Leo, a lion.**"

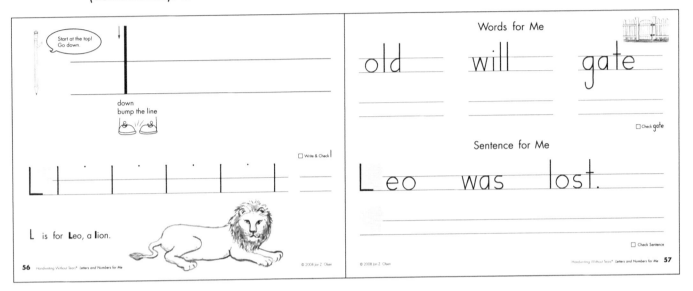

Multisensory Activities

Imaginary Writing
Use *Air Writing* to demonstrate **l**. Children follow along in the air. See page 52 of this guide.

Finger Trace Models Step-by-Step

Letter Size and Place
L and **l** are different, but both begin above the lines.

Say the step-by-step directions for **l** while children finger trace each step.

Copy and Check l

Demonstrate **l**, saying the step-by-step directions. Children watch, then copy **l**s.
☑ Check letter: start, steps, bump

Copy and Check Words

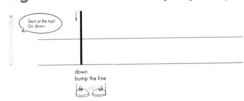

Demonstrate **gate**
Emphasize that the letters are close.
Children watch, then copy.
☑ Check word: size, placement, closeness

Copy and Check Words and Sentences

Demonstrate **Leo was lost.**
Emphasize capitalization, word spacing, and period.
☑ Check sentence: capital, spaces, end

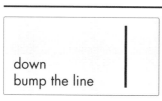

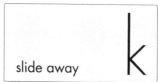

k   down / bump the line | kick!   slide away

Get Started   Say, "Turn to page 58. This is lowercase **k**. Watch me write lowercase **k**. I make it like this (demonstrate). Let's read this sentence: **K is for kangaroos.**"

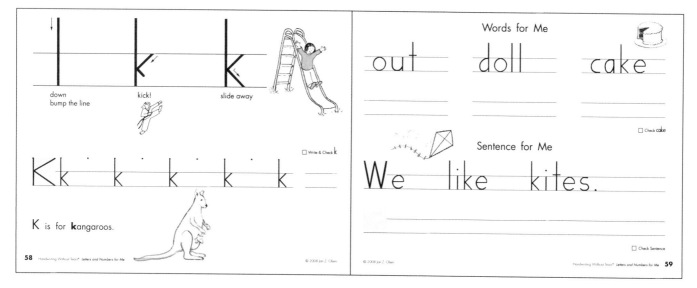

Multisensory Activities

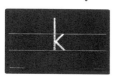

Wet–Dry–Try
Use the Blackboard with Double Lines. See page 48 of this guide.

Mr. Kaye ← / ← you

Letter Story
See page 58 of this guide.

Finger Trace Models Step-by-Step

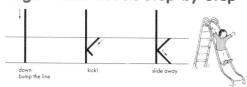

down / bump the line   kick!   slide away

Say the step-by-step directions for **k** while children finger trace each step.

Copy and Check k

Demonstrate **k**, saying the step-by-step directions. Children watch, then copy **k**s.
☑ Check letter: start, steps, bump

Copy and Check Words

Demonstrate **cake**
Emphasize that the letters are close. Children watch, then copy.
☑ Check word: size, placement, closeness

Copy and Check Words and Sentences

Demonstrate **We like kites.**
Emphasize capitalization, word spacing, and period.
☑ Check sentence: capital, spaces, end

Tips
- Encourage the 'hi-yaaaaa' when writing the kick stroke so it's a continuous stroke.
- Use the *Rock, Rap, Tap & Learn* CD, *Sentence Song*, Track 7.

Teach

| slide down | \ | slide down |  |

Get Started Say, "Turn to page 60. This is lowercase **y**. Watch me write lowercase **y**. I make it like this (demonstrate). Let's read this sentence: **Y is for yogurt.**"

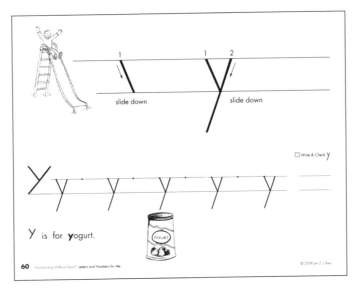

Multisensory Activities

Music and Movement
Use the *Rock, Rap, Tap & Learn* CD, *Diagonals*, Track 5. Have children trace diagonal strokes in the air.

Finger Trace Models Step-by-Step

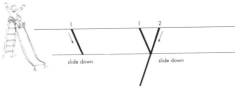

Copy and Check y

Imaginary Writing
Use a laser and trace letter **y** on the board or on an easel. Children follow along in the air. See page 53 of this guide.

Say the step-by-step directions for **y** while children finger trace each step.

Demonstrate **y** saying the step-by-step directions. Children watch, then copy **y**s.
☑ Check letter: start, steps, bump

Tips
- Teach that **Y** and **y** are the same. They're just in different positions.
- Teach that **y** goes below the line.
- You or your student may choose another style for capital **Y** – **Y**.
- If student slides the stroke the wrong way, count very slowly. One.......Two.............Which comes first? One. Make one slide down first. Slide the way the boy in the picture is sliding.
- Check Your Teaching, page 146 of this guide.

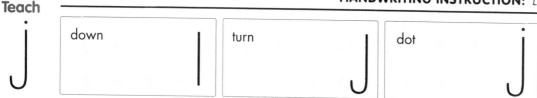

J | down | turn | dot

Get Started   Say, "Turn to page 61. This is lowercase **j**. Watch me write lowercase **j**. I make it like this (demonstrate). Let's read this sentence: **J is for juice.**"

Multisensory Activities

Wet–Dry–Try
Use the Blackboard with Double Lines. See page 48 of this guide.

Imaginary Writing
Use *My Teacher Writes* to demonstrate **j**. Children follow along in the air. See page 52 of this guide.

Say the step-by-step directions for **j** while children finger trace each step.

Finger Trace Models Step-by-Step

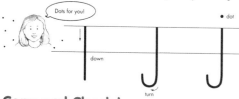

Copy and Check j

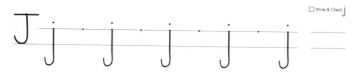

Demonstrate **j**, saying the step-by-step directions. Children watch, then copy **j**s.
☑ Check letter: start, steps, bump

Tips

- Teach that **J** and **j** are similar. Point out the differences. They start in different places. They have different tops.
- Teach that **j** goes below the line.
- **J** and **j** turn the same direction as lowercase **g**.
- If **J** and **j** curve too much, make a ruler-straight line down. Turn only at the bottom.

Take your students to *Diver School*, Track 18, and teach them the diver letters. The diver letters are **p r n m h b**. They all start with a diver motion: dive down, swim up, and over.

Diver Letters' School

Boys and girls, welcome to diver school
Stand up and get ready

When you dive in a pool
It makes you feel so cool
When you dive in a pool
It makes you feel so cool

You have to stand up straight, oh yeah (2X)
And you shake, shake, shake, oh yeah (2X)
You put your arms up straight, way up (2X)
And then you WAIT, WAIT, WAIT!
And then you wait, wait, wait…

Are you ready…are you ready?
Here we goooooooooo….
Deep breath

Dive down, swim up and over
What fun!
Dive down, swim up, and over
We're not done!

Dive down, swim up, and over
You better!
Dive down, swim up, and over
In diver letters!

Let's try it faster!
Are you ready?
Here we goooooooooo…
Deep breath

Dive down, swim up, and over
What fun!
Dive down, swim up, and over
We're not done!

Dive down, swim up, and over
You better!
Dive down, swim up, and over
in diver letters!

Tips
- Toss out pretend swimming suits to your class to put on.
- Bring in your own whistle to whistle with the CD.

| P | dive down | l | swim up and over | r | around bump | p |

Get Started   Say, "Turn to page 62. This is lowercase **p**. Watch me write lowercase **p**. I make it like this (demonstrate). Let's read this sentence: **P is for puppies.**"

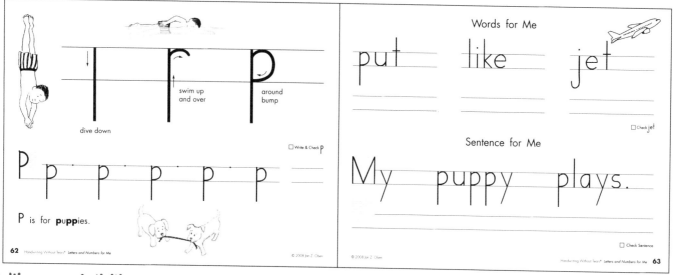

Multisensory Activities

Imaginary Writing
Follow the ball and Air Write **p**. Children follow along in the air. See page 53 of this guide.

Finger Trace Models Step-by-Step

Copy and Check p

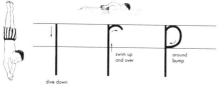

Copy and Check Words

Copy and Check Words and Sentence

Letter Size and Place
P is tall. Lowercase **p** is descending. See page 54 of this guide.

P   **p**

Say the step-by-step directions for **p** while children finger trace each step.

Demonstrate **p**, saying the step-by-step directions. Children watch, then copy **p**s.
☑ Check letter: start, steps, bump

Demonstrate **jet**
Emphasize that the letters are close.
☑ Check word: size, placement, closeness

Demonstrate **My puppy plays.**
Emphasize capitalization, word spacing, and period.
☑ Check sentence: capital, spaces, end

Tip
• Capital **P** has been taught with two strokes. Your students may make **P** with a continuous stroke.

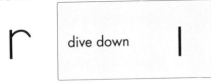 dive down | swim up and over ⌐

Get Started Say, "Turn to page 64. This is lowercase **r**. Watch me write lowercase **r**. I make it like this (demonstrate). Let's read this sentence: **R is for rain.**"

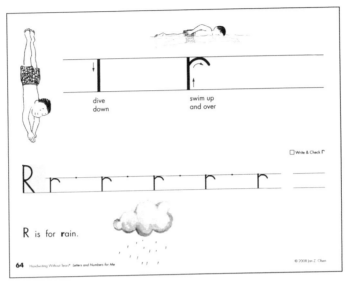

Multisensory Activities

Music and Movement
Use the *Rock, Rap, Tap & Learn* CD, *Diver Letters' School*, Track 18. See page 128 of this guide.

Wet–Dry–Try
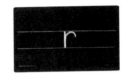
Use the Blackboard with Double Lines. See page 48 of this guide.

Finger Trace Models Step-by-Step

Say the step-by-step directions for **r** while children finger trace each step.

Copy and Check r
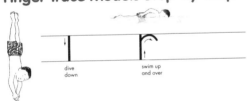

Demonstrate **r** saying the step-by-step directions. Children watch, then copy **r**s.
☑ Check letter: start, steps, bump

Tips
- Capital **R** has been taught with two strokes. Your students may make **R** with a continuous stroke.
- If re-tracing is a problem, tell them the pencil must retrace until it gets to the line and can swim over.
- Children may draw a rainbow and add raindrops.

n	dive down	l	swim up and over	r	one hump down	n

Get Started   Say, "Turn to page 65. This is lowercase **n**. Watch me write lowercase **n**. I make it like this (demonstrate.) Let's read this sentence: **N is for newspaper.**"

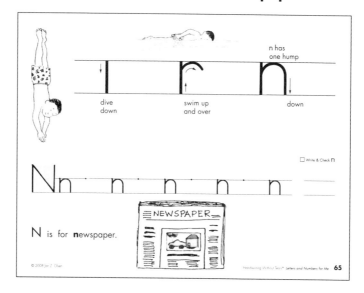

Multisensory Activities

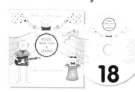

18

Music and Movement
Use the *Rock, Rap, Tap & Learn* CD, *Diver Letters' School*, Track 18. See page 128 of this guide.

N   n

Letter Size and Place
N is tall and **n** is small. Lowercase **n** fits between the lines.

Finger Trace Models Step-by-Step

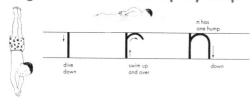

Say the step-by-step directions for **n** while children finger trace each step.

Copy and Check n

☐ Write & Check n

Demonstrate **n**, saying the step-by-step directions. Children watch, then copy **n**s.
☑ Check letter: start, steps, bump

Tips
- Be sure the **n** is started on the mid line.
- If **n** finishes with a slide, teach that **n** comes straight down. No sliding allowed.
- If re-tracing is a problem, explain that the pencil must retrace until it gets to the top line and can swim over.

m | start with n | n | swim up and over | m | down | m

Get Started Say, "Turn to page 66. This is lowercase **m**. Watch me write lowercase **m**. I make it like this (demonstrate). Let's read this sentence: **M is for mouse.**"

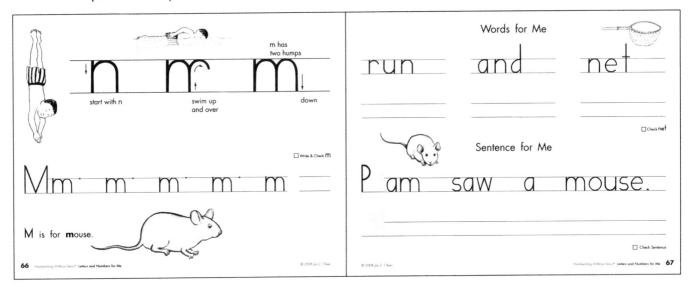

Multisensory Activities

Music and Movement
Use the *Rock, Rap, Tap & Learn* CD, *Diver Letters' School, Track 18*. See page 128 of this guide.

Letter Story
See page 59 of this guide.

Finger Trace Models Step-by-Step

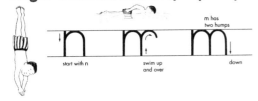

Say the step-by-step directions for **m** while children finger trace each step.

Copy and Check m

Mm m m m m

Demonstrate **m**, saying the step-by-step directions.
Children watch, then copy **m**s.
☑ Check letter: start, steps, bump

Copy and Check Words

run   and   net

Demonstrate **net**
Emphasize that the letters are close.
Children watch, then copy.
☑ Check word: size, placement, closeness

Copy and Check Words and Sentence

Pam saw a mouse.

Demonstrate **Pam saw a mouse**.
Emphasize capitalization, word spacing, and period.
☑ Check sentence: capital, spaces, end

Teach

dive down	swim up and over	down
 | 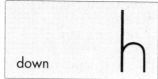 |

Get Started   Say, "Turn to page 68. This is lowercase **h**. Watch me write lowercase **h**. I make it like this (demonstrate). Let's read this sentence: **H is for hair.**"

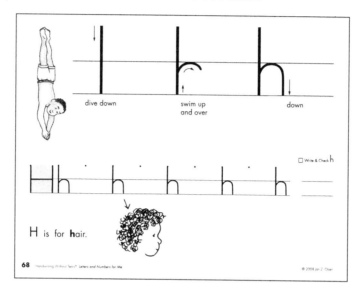

Multisensory Activities

Music and Movement
Use the *Rock, Rap, Tap & Learn* CD, *Diver Letters' School, Track 18*. See page 128 of this guide.

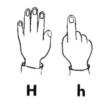

H   h

Letter Size and Place
H and **h** are both tall. See page 54 of this guide.

Finger Trace Models Step-by-Step

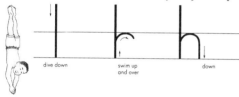

Say the step-by-step directions for **h** while children finger trace each step.

Copy and Check h

Demonstrate **h** saying the step-by-step directions. Children watch, then copy **h**s.
☑ Check letter: start, steps, bump

Tips
- If **h** is too short, emphasize the **h** as a high dive that starts way up in the air.
- If **h** finishes with a slide, teach that **h** comes straight down. No sliding allowed.
- If retracing is a problem, the pencil must retrace until it gets to the top line and can swim over.

Teach

 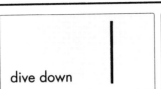

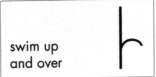 dive down	swim up and over	 around bump	

Get Started   Say, "Turn to page 69. This is lowercase **b**. Watch me write lowercase **b**. I make it like this (demonstrate). Let's read this sentence: **B is for backpack.**"

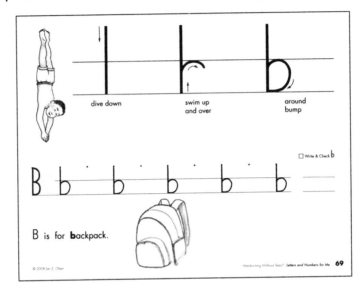

Multisensory Activities

Music and Movement
Use the *Rock, Rap, Tap & Learn* CD, *Diver Letters' School, Track 18.* See 128 of this guide.

Letter Story
See page 58 of this guide.

Finger Trace Models Step-by-Step

Say the step-by-step directions for **b** while children finger trace each step.

Copy and Check b

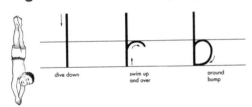

Demonstrate **b** saying the step-by-step directions. Children watch, then copy **b**s.
☑ Check letter: start, steps, bump

Tips

- To help children who come to you with **b** and **d** confusion, teach them **b** by starting with **h** and teach **d** by starting with **c**.
- Check Your Teaching, page 146 of this guide.

f

| up |
| down |

cross

Get Started   Say, "Turn to page 70. This is lowercase **f**. Watch me write lowercase **f**. I make it like this (demonstrate). Let's read this sentence: **F is for firetruck.**"

Multisensory Activities

7

Music and Movement
Use the *Rock, Rap, Tap & Learn* CD,
Sentence Song, Track 7.

Letter Story
See page 58 of this guide.

Finger Trace Models Step-by-Step

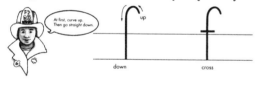

Say the step-by-step directions for **f**
while children finger trace each step.

Copy and Check f

Demonstrate **f**, saying the step-by-step directions.
Children watch, then copy **f**s.
☑ Check letter: start, steps, bump

Copy and Check Words

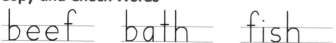

Demonstrate **fish**
Emphasize that the letters are close.
Children watch, then copy.
☑ Check word: size, placement, closeness

Copy and Check Words and Sentence

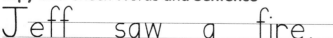

Demonstrate **Jeff saw a fire**.
Emphasize capitalization, word spacing, and period.
☑ Check sentence: capital, spaces, end

Teach

| q | Magic c | C | up like a helicopter bump | O | back down | q | U turn | q |

Get Started Say, "Turn to page 72. This is lowercase **q**. Watch me write lowercase **q**. I make it like this (demonstrate). Let's read this sentence: **Q is for queen.**"

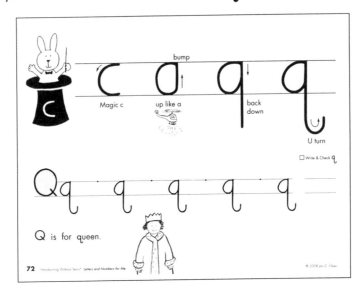

Multisensory Activities

Voices
Demonstrate **q** on the board/easel using the Voices activity, page 55 of this guide.

Letter Story
For children who confuse **g** with **q**, teach the Letter Story. See page 59 of this guide.

Finger Trace Models Step-by-Step

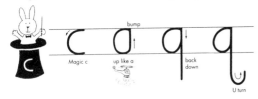

Say the step-by-step directions for **q** while children finger trace each step.

Copy and Check q

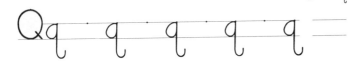

Demonstrate **q** saying the step-by-step directions. Children watch, then copy **q**s.
☑ Check letter: start, steps, bump

Tips

- The letter **q** is always followed by **u**. Teach children to finish **q** with a u-turn so they can practice writing the next letter in the word.
- If children reverse **q**, teach them the letter story.
- Children may color the queen and add a king.

 slide down \ slide down

Get Started Say, "Turn to page 73. This is lowercase **x**. Watch me write lowercase **x**. I make it like this (demonstrate). Let's read this sentence: **X is for xylophone.**"

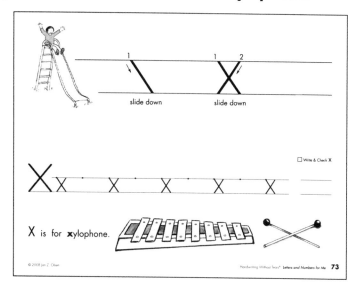

Multisensory Activities

Music and Movement
Use the *Rock, Rap, Tap & Learn* CD.
Have children sing *Diagonals*, Track 5.

Imaginary Writing
Use *Air Writing* to demonstrate
x. See page 52 of this guide.

Finger Trace Models Step-by-Step

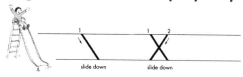

Say the step-by-step directions for **x**
while children finger trace each step.

Copy and Check x

Demonstrate **x**, saying the step-by-step directions.
Children watch, then copy **x**s.
☑ Check letter: start, steps, bump

Tip
• If diagonal lines are a problem, have children finger trace the slide illustration on their page.

| Z | go across | — | slide down | 7 | go across | Z |

Get Started Say, "Turn to page 74. This is lowercase **z**. Watch me write lowercase **z**. I make it like this (demonstrate). Let's read this sentence: **Z is for zipper.**"

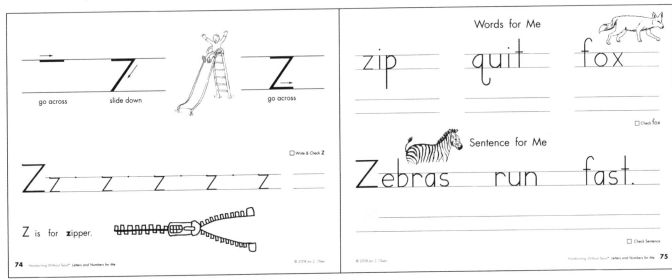

Multisensory Activity

Music and Movement
Use the *Rock, Rap, Tap & Learn* CD. *Sliding Down to the End of the Alphabet,* Track 15. Stand up and slide down to the alphabet for letters **v w x y z**.

Finger Trace Models Step-by-Step

Say the step-by-step directions for **z** while children finger trace each step.

Copy and Check z

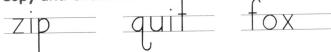

Demonstrate **z**, saying the step-by-step directions. Children watch, then copy **z**s.
☑ Check letter: start, steps, bump

Copy and Check Words

zip   quit   fox

Demonstrate **fox**
Emphasize that the letters are close.
Children watch, then copy.
☑ Check word: size, placement, closeness

Copy and Check Words and Sentence

Demonstrate **Zebras run fast.**
Emphasize capitalization, word spacing, and period.
☑ Check sentence: capital, spaces, end

Tip

• Check Your Teaching, page 146 of this guide.

Activity Page – LABEL MAT MAN™

Forget Superman! Mat Man is the man for you and your kindergarten students. He can teach them about drawing, doing things in order, body parts, etc. On this page, he'll help you teach labels.

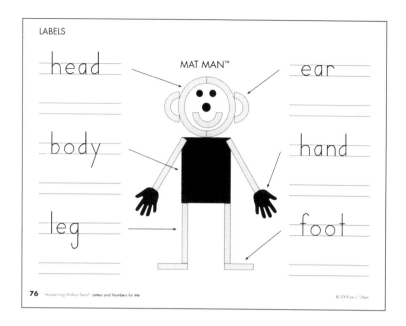

Tell them...

This page has a picture of Mat Man and words. Guess what those words are doing? They are naming Mat Man's body parts. Those words are labels.

How do I teach this?
Show children how words work as labels.

Explain	The labels are near Mat Man's parts. Can you find the word **head**? It is at the top. Follow the arrow to Mat Man's head. Point to your head. Where is the word **foot**?
Continue	Reading and pointing to all words and body parts.

Demonstrate writing the words.

At the board:

Draw	Stick figure Mat Man.
Write	**head** at the top left, placing it as if on the page.
	— Wait for children to copy
Continue	Writing each part.

The FINE Print is a play on words with the name of Edith Fine, a contributor to some of the linguistic insights scattered throughout this guide. In "The Fine Print," you'll find content ranging from advanced instruction to tips that are just for fun. Edith Fine is an accomplished author of children's books on teaching elementary school students grammar.

The FINE Print   Labels are an important part of your room and your school. It's fun to go on a label hunt or to add labels to the parts and objects in your room.

Activity Page – PUNCTUATION

When we talk, we do not use punctuation. Our voices and faces help people understand what we're saying. Use this lesson to teach students how to use punctuation and how to write on other styles of lines. See the Hand Activity on page 54 of this guide to help reinforce letter size and place.

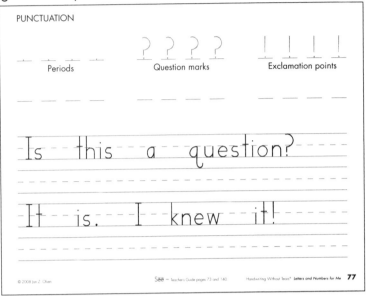

Tell them...

This page has different styles of lines. Lines keep our writing straight. They help us write an even size. The double lines are like the ones in this book. Sometimes our worksheets use other lines. We can write on all different types.

How do I teach this?

Demonstrate the marks.

At the board: Write/Say

. This is a period. Make a dot.

? This is a question mark. Start at the top, little curve, little line down, dot.

! This is an exclamation point. Start at the top, big line down, dot.

Draw lines on the board and explain their names and uses.

At the board: Draw — Baseline
Say — This is a baseline. Only the descending letters **g j y p q** can go below the baseline.

At the board: Add — Solid and broken mid-line above the baseline
Say — This is a midline. This one is solid. This one is broken. They are both midlines. All the small letters fit in this middle space.
a c e i m n o r s u v w x z

At the board: Add — Top line only above the dotted midline
Say — Paper that uses a dotted midline always has a top line. It looks like this. Tall letters **b h k l t** start there.

For more information on line generalization visit **www.hwtears.com/click**.

Activity Page – MAGIC C LETTERS

With this page, you can change bad habits, like starting at the bottom, going the wrong way, or floating letters. The Magic C Bunny keeps the name of the letter a secret until the children trace Magic C. Then he tells them the name of the letter to make. See how helpful this lesson is!

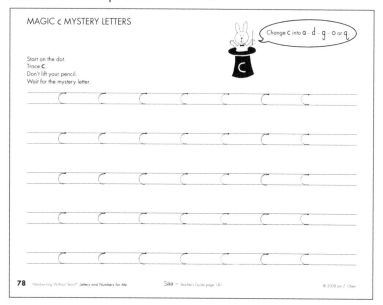

Tell them...

The Magic C Bunny has a mystery for you. He wants you to trace Magic c first and wait at the bottom of **c**. Then, he'll tell you the mystery letter.

Before   After Magic c Mystery Letters

How do I teach this?

Preview turning c c c c into a d g o

Say	Write **c c c c** on double lines
	Trace each **c** before changing it to **a d g o**

Pretend the Magic C Bunny is telling the children what to do

Say	Magic C Bunny wants you to:
	• Trace the first **c** and wait at the bottom of **c**
	• Change **c** into **d**. (Or **a g o** or leave as **c**)
	• Repeat six times to finish the line
	• Do one line each day

Activity Page – RHYMING WORDS

Here is a page to help children associate **h** and **b**. Letters **h** and **b** start the same way. They are both Diver Letters. Because children seldom reverse letter **h**, thinking of **h** and **b** together prevents **b** reversals and **b/d** confusion. Teach them to think of **h** for honey and then **b** for honeybee. The rhyming words are another bonus for developing both reading and handwriting skills.

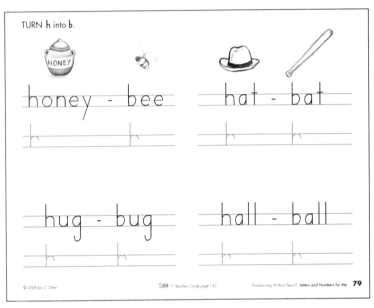

Tell them...
This page has words that start with letter **h** and rhyming words that start with letter **b**. Letters **h** and **b** start the same way. They are both Diver Letters, in fact, they are high dive letters. They start up high.

How do I teach this?
Review h and b with Diver Letter activity
Note: Do this air tracing activity while facing the class. Make your Diver Letters swim over to the your left so that they'll be right for your children to trace in the air.

Say/Move	Look at me. Point to this ball. Follow it with your finger as it moves.
	Start high. This is a high dive letter.
	Dive down, swim up, and over ...and down.
	That is **h**.
Repeat	Let's do **h** again. This time, I'll have a surprise at the end.
	Start high. Letter **h** is a high dive letter.
	Dive down, come up, swim over and down.
	That makes **h** for a .....honey bee.
	Did you see me? I turned the **h** into **b**.

Teach rhyming words
At the board: Preview   How to write a dash
                 Write/spell   **honey – bee**
                 Explain   The ending letters are different but the **E** sound is the same.
                 — Wait for children to copy.

                 Write/spell   **hat - bat**
                 Explain   Both words end with **at**. They rhyme.
                 — Wait for children to copy.
                 Repeat with   **hug - bug** / Both words end with **ug**. They rhyme.

Activity Page – PARAGRAPH

This page is really at a first grade level. But your children have all the basic skills to do it if you spend a couple of days on it.

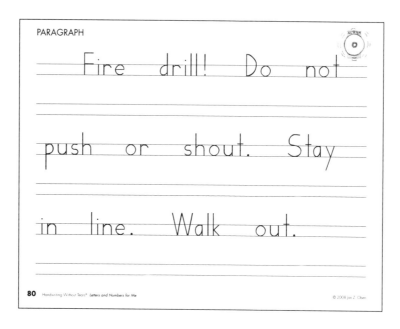

Tell them...
Look at this page! It is not a word page. It is not a sentence page. This is a paragraph page. It is really first grade work, but we are going to do it.

How do I teach this?
Explain the basics as they copy the paragraph.

1. **Paragraphs have a topic.**

Read	Paragraph aloud together.
Ask	What is the topic? What is this paragraph about?
Say	All of the sentences are about a fire drill. We know about fire drills.

2. **Paragraphs are indented.**

	Explain	We move over a big space BEFORE we write. That is called indenting.
At the board:	Indent/Write	**Fire drill!**
	Explain	Capitalize **F** because it is the first letter of the first word. Leave a space after **Fire**. Use an **!** because these are strong words. **Fire drill!** is not a sentence. We can use it as an exclamation.
	— Wait for children to copy.	

3. **Paragraphs have sentences.**

At the board:	Write	**Do not push or shout.**
	Explain	Sentences may start on one line and go to the next line.
		Sentences do three other important things.
		1. Sentences start with a capital
		2. Sentences have space between words.
		3. Sentences end with a period. (Questions with a question mark, exclamations with an exclamation point)
	— Wait for children to copy. Save the rest of the page for tomorrow.	
At the board:	Write	**Stay**
		in line. Walk out.
	Explain	Some sentences take more than one line to write and some just take one line.

Activity Page – POEM

For centuries, nursery rhymes have been part of early education. Here's a spin off of Little Miss Muffet.

Tell them...

Little Miss Muffet sat on a tuffet, eating her curds and whey, Along came a spider, Who sat down beside her, And frightened Miss Muffet away! Then see if they can say the rhyme with you. Now, whatever is a tuffet? Curds and whey?

How do I teach this?
Use this nursery rhyme/poem page to teach sequence.

Explain	In the beginning	She was sitting and eating.
	In the middle	A spider came.
	At the end	She was so scared, she ran away.

Teach poem basics.

Read	Title and poem
Explain	1. Poems have titles. **A Spider** is the title. A title is the name of the poem.
	2. Poems have lines. Lines start with capitals but they are not sentences.
	3. Poems use rhyme. The ends of the lines rhyme: **dear - near - here**

Teach handwriting skills for poems.

At the board: Write **Oh dear!**
  Explain 1. Capitalize **O** because **Oh** is the first word on the line.
  2. Leave a space after **Oh**. (space between words)
  3. This line ends with an **!** because **Oh dear!** shows strong feeling. Put your hands on your faces and say **Oh!** Your mouth makes a surprised O shape.
— Wait for children to copy.
  Write **Spider near,**
  Explain 1. Capitalize **S** because **Spider** is the first word on the line.
  2. Leave a space after **Spider**. (space between words)
  3. This line ends with a comma. Poem lines can end in commas, or even with nothing.
— Wait for children to copy.
  Write **Out of here!**
  Explain 1. Capitalize **O** because **Out** is the first word of the line.
  2. I leave a space after **Out** and after **of** (space between words).
  3. This line ends with an **!** because **Out of here!** shows strong feeling.
— Wait for children to copy.

Activity Page – SENTENCES

Before they come to kindergarten, children know what animals say! Now you're going to use those familiar sounds to teach them how to complete sentences.

Tell them...
Look at the pictures. What do pigs say? What do ducks say? What do sheep say? What do cows say? Guess what? Those words are in the bubbles. We are going to use those words to finish the sentences. I'm also going to show you how to write on one line.

How do I teach this?
Show how to complete sentences, write commas, and end sentences with periods. Demonstrate writing on one line.

At the board:	Write	**Pigs say**
	Ask	What do pigs say? Where do you see **oink, oink?**
	Write	**Pigs say oink, oink.**
	Say	I use a comma after the first oink. I make it like this (demonstrate). I end the sentence with a period.
	— Wait while children finish the sentence.	
At the board:	Write	**Ducks say**
	Ask	What do ducks say? Where do you see **quack, quack?**
	Write	**Ducks say quack, quack.**
	Say	I use a comma after the first quack. I make it like this (demonstrate).
	Say	I end the sentence with a period.
	— Wait while children finish the sentence.	
At the board:	Write	**Sheep say**
	Ask	What do sheep say? Where do you see **baa, baa?**
	Write	**Sheep say baa, baa.**
	Say	I use a comma after the first baa. I make it like this (demonstrate).
	Say	I end the sentence with a period.
	— Wait while children finish the sentence.	
At the board:	Write	**Cows say**
	Ask	What do cows say? Where do you see **moo?**
	Write	**Cows say moo.**
	Say	I end the sentence with a period.
	— Wait while children finish the sentence.	

✓ Check Your Teaching

This unique strategy allows you to Check Your Teaching as you go, or Check Your Teaching at the end of it all. Because handwriting is taught through direct instruction, you can check if you did a good job teaching children letters. We have separated these mini-tests by letter group. You can give the tests to a class, but we suggest small groups or one-on-one. It's best when you can watch students form their letters.

Directions:
1. On a blank sheet of paper, draw a single line.
2. Ask the child to print the word for the letter group you are checking (see below).
3. Spell the word(s) for the child.
4. Check their letters and spacing.
5. If there are problems, go back and review letters with the child.

To Check: **Child Writes:**

✓ c o s v w   cows

✓ a d g t   cat dog

✓ l k y j u i e   I like you.

✓ p r n m h b   run jump bath

✓ f q x z   fax quiz

To download a "Check Your Teaching" worksheet to give these mini-test by letter group or combined, visit **www.hwtears.com/click**.

NUMBERS

Multisensory Activities for Numbers

You will teach numbers similarly to how you teach capital letters. You can use a variety of multisensory activities to support your teaching. Our three favorites are listed below. They combine to make a foolproof method of teaching numbers so children won't reverse them.

Wet–Dry–Try

Teacher's Part	Student's Part		

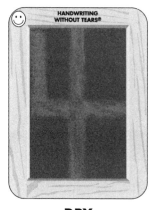 

Teacher demonstrates correct number formation.

WET
• Wet a Little Sponge Cube.
• Squeeze it out.
• Trace the number with the sponge.
• Wet your finger and trace again.

DRY
• Crumple a little paper towel.
• Dry the number a few times.
• Gently blow for final drying.

TRY
• Take a Little Chalk Bit.
• Use it to write the number.

Gray Blocks

Gray Blocks are an easy transition from the Slate Chalkboard. Refer to them as "tiny pictures of the Slate," and children will transfer the Slate Chalkboard concepts beautifully. You can purchase Gray Block paper at www.hwtears.com.

1 2 3 4 5 6 7 8 9 10

Door Tracing

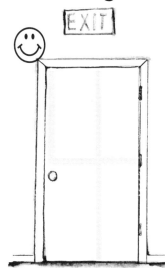

The smiley face concepts are good for preventing and correcting reversals. This is a multisensory activity for large body movements. Pretend the door is a large slate or a large Gray Block and trace numbers in it. You can use a laser too. Refer to page 50 for further direction.

Try this fun game! Play the Boss of the Door. Students take turns tracing numbers in the door and guessing one another's numbers. To make math activities a little more exciting, challenge students to trace a number and have another student give a basic math question that makes that answer (e.g., the student would trace **9** and another would say, "8 + 1").

big line down

Get Started Say, "Turn to page 84. This is **I**. Watch me. I make it like this (demonstrate **I** on paper or board). Let's read these sentences, 'I can write **I**. I can count **I**.' Look, (teacher points) one whale."

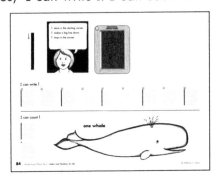

Finger Trace Model Step-by-Step

Say the step-by-step directions while tracing.
Children watch, then trace **I**.

Copy 1

Say the step-by-step directions while demonstrating.
Children watch, then copy **I**s.

Teach

big curve   little line across

Get Started Say, "Turn to page 85. This is **2**. Watch me. I make it like this (demonstrate **2** on paper or board). Let's read these sentences, 'I can write **2**. I can count to **2**.' Look, (teacher points) two alligators."

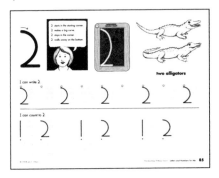

Finger Trace Model Step-by-Step

Say the step-by-step directions while tracing.
Children watch, then trace **2**.

Copy 2

Say the step-by-step directions while demonstrating
Children watch, then copy **2**s.

Teach

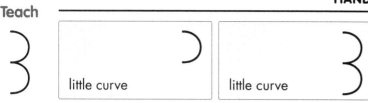

little curve	little curve

Get Started Say, "Turn to page 86. This is **3**. Watch me. I make it like this (demonstrate **3** on paper or board). Let's read these sentences, 'I can write **3**. I can count to **3**.' Look, (teacher points) three fish."

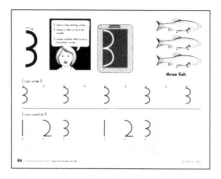

Finger Trace Model Step-by-Step

Say the step-by-step directions while tracing. Children watch, then trace **3**.

Copy 3

Say the step-by-step directions while demonstrating. Children watch, then copy **3**s.

Teach

little line down	little line across	big line down

Get Started Say, "Turn to page 87. This is **4**. Watch me. I make it like this (demonstrate **4** on paper or board). Let's read these sentences, 'I can write **4**. I can count to **4**.' Look, (teacher points) four snowman."

Finger Trace Model Step-by-Step

Say the step-by-step directions while tracing. Children watch, then trace **4**.

Copy 4

Say the step-by-step directions while demonstrating. Children watch, then copy **4**s.

Teach

5

I	little line down

5	little curve

5	jump little line across

Get Started   Say, "Turn to page 88. This is **5**. Watch me. I make it like this (demonstrate **5** on paper or board). Let's read these sentences, 'I can write **5**. I can count to **5**.' Look, (teacher points) five umbrellas."

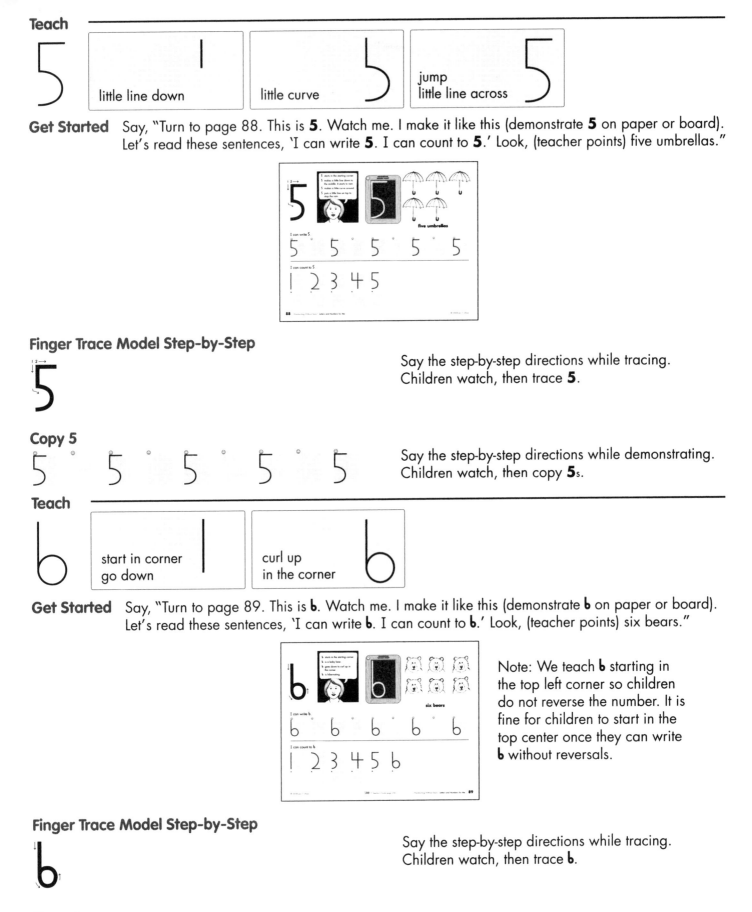

Finger Trace Model Step-by-Step

5

Say the step-by-step directions while tracing. Children watch, then trace **5**.

Copy 5

5   5   5   5   5

Say the step-by-step directions while demonstrating. Children watch, then copy **5**s.

Teach

6

I	start in corner go down

6	curl up in the corner

Get Started   Say, "Turn to page 89. This is **6**. Watch me. I make it like this (demonstrate **6** on paper or board). Let's read these sentences, 'I can write **6**. I can count to **6**.' Look, (teacher points) six bears."

Note: We teach **6** starting in the top left corner so children do not reverse the number. It is fine for children to start in the top center once they can write **6** without reversals.

Finger Trace Model Step-by-Step

6

Say the step-by-step directions while tracing. Children watch, then trace **6**.

Copy 6

6   6   6   6   6

Say the step-by-step directions while demonstrating. Children watch, then copy **6**s.

Teach

7

| little line across | big line slide down 7 |

Get Started Say, "Turn to page 90. This is **7**. Watch me. I make it like this (demonstrate **7** on paper or board). Let's read these sentences, 'I can write **7**. I can count to **7**.' Look, (teacher points) seven potato plants."

Finger Trace Model Step-by-Step

7

Say the step-by-step directions while tracing.
Children watch, then trace **7**.

Copy 7

7   7   7   7   7

Say the step-by-step directions while demonstrating.
Children watch, then copy **7**s.

Teach

8

| begin with S S | back up to the top 8 |

Get Started Say, "Turn to page 91. This is **8**. Watch me. I make it like this (demonstrate **8** on paper or board). Let's read these sentences, 'I can write **8**. I can count to **8**.' Look, (teacher points) eight spiders."

Finger Trace Model Step-by-Step

8

Say the step-by-step directions while tracing.
Children watch, then trace **8**.

Copy 8

Say the step-by-step directions while demonstrating.
Children watch, then copy **8**s.

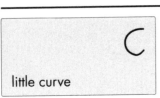 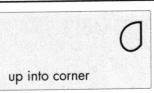 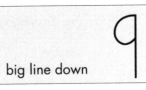

little curve   up into corner   big line down

Get Started   Say, "Turn to page 92. This is **9**. Watch me. I make it like this (demonstrate **9** on paper or board). Let's read these sentences, 'I can write **9**. I can count to **9**.' Look, (teacher points) nine numbers."

Finger Trace Model Step-by-Step

Say the step-by-step directions while tracing. Children watch, then trace **9**.

Copy 9

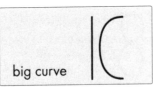 

Say the step-by-step directions while demonstrating. Children watch, then copy **9**s.

Teach

big line   big curve   go around

Get Started   Say, "Turn to page 93. This is **10**. Watch me. I make it like this (demonstrate **10** on paper or board). Let's read these sentences, 'I can write **10**. I can count to **10**.' Look, (teacher points) ten balloons."

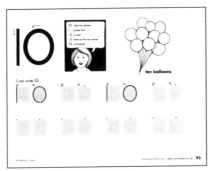

Finger Trace Model Step-by-Step

Say the step-by-step directions while tracing. Children watch, then trace **10**.

Copy 10

Say the step-by-step directions while demonstrating. Children watch, then copy **10**s.

Activity Page – NUMBERS FOR ME

Children will like this review page. It's fun to see all the numbers they've just done.

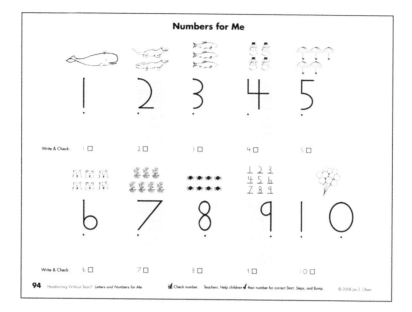

Tell them...

You have finished all the numbers up to **10**. This is a review page. It has the pictures and numbers from the **10** pages all on one page.

How do I teach this?

Explain   Look at the pictures and numbers in the first row.
                 You can count and you can write each number in the Gray Block.
                 Start every number on the dot. Numbers **1 2 3 4 5** start in the starting corner.
– Wait while students copy.
Look at the pictures and numbers in the next row. They are numbers **6 7 8 9 10**.
Start every number on the dot.
6 and **7** start in the starting corner.
8 starts at the top center of the Gray Block.
9 has its own corner.
10 uses different starting places for the one and the zero.
1 starts in the starting corner.
0 start at the top center of the Gray Block

How do I help children with number reversals?

Despite your good teaching and these workbook pages, some children forget what they've learned when they are using worksheets or writing numbers on other papers. Use this friendly strategy:
    1. Check arithmetic or counting papers.
    2. Mark only one reversal per paper. Mark the lowest number. Ignore all other reversals.
    3. Show the child how to make the one reversed number correctly with the Slate or Gray Block.
Gradually, all reversals will be eliminated. You will always teach the lowest number and it will get all the help it needs. With this technique, you can easily eliminate all reversals.

HANDWRITING ADVICE
Identifying Handwriting Difficulties

As discussed in the beginning of this guide, your students may come with very different levels of writing proficiency. This section is especially important for those who enter your room less prepared. Think in terms of the eight skills required for speed and legibility (page 7). If you break the handwriting processes into these skills, it is easier to identify and correct difficulties. Use the tips below to guide your approach when helping a child who is behind in handwriting. Often the printing skills are fine, but the physical approach to handwriting or the child's interest in self-correction may need some adjustments. If you feel the difficulty stems from something other than just a lack of instruction, consult an occupational therapist.

Below are some of the things to look for to identify where a child needs help. On the pages that follow, we include strategies for addressing specific difficulties.

PHYSICAL APPROACH
Handedness
- Switches hands while writing
- Switches hands between activities

Pencil Grip
- Holds pencil vertically
- Wraps thumb around fingers
- Uses an awkward grip
- Holds pencil with an open hand

Pencil Pressure
- Presses too hard
- Presses too lightly

Paper Placement
- Positions paper incorrectly for handedness

Posture
- Slouches in chair
- Has head on table
- Slumps

Helper Hand
- Moves paper when writing
- Places helping hand incorrectly

SELF CORRECTION
Erasing/Editing
- Erases too much
- Works carelessly

PRINTING SKILLS
Memory
- Misses letters or numbers in assignments
- Confuses capital and lowercase letters
- Writes unidentifiable letters/numbers

Orientation
- Reverses letters or numbers

Placement
- Misplaces certain letters or numbers
- Uses wrong lines

Size
- Makes letter size too big for grade level papers

Start
- Writes letters/numbers from the bottom
- Starts with the wrong part or on the wrong side

Sequence
- Forms letters that are not standard
- Makes letter strokes out of order

Spacing
- Puts too much space between letters in words
- Runswordstogether

Control
- Makes misshapen letters/numbers

Remediating Handwriting Difficulties

The remediation strategies here can help you correct handwriting difficulties. In addition, parents often ask about ways they too can assist their child. This section gives you remediation tips and information for parents.

When facilitating handwriting remediation, remember the following:

Notice what's right: Recognition of what's right is encouraging and should come before any suggestions or corrections. You can give this easy handwriting check to your students to see if they learned what you taught them. Use it after teaching each letter group, or give it to students all at once to see what they already know and what they need.

On a blank sheet of paper, draw a single horizontal line and have the child write:

cows
cat   dog
I like you.
run jump bath
fax quiz

Make sure you mark each letter with numbers and arrows to show how it was made. You may spell the words for children.

Keep practice short: Ten or fifteen minutes is long enough. You want the child's full attention and optimum effort during the lesson. Then end the lesson while it's still going well or the minute you've lost the child's interest.

Use imitation: What is imitation? It is watching someone do something first, then doing it yourself. With imitation, the child has the opportunity to see how a letter is written; to see the actual movements which were responsible for making the mark. Then the child can associate the mark with the movement that produced it. This is crucial because we are as concerned with how a letter is formed as we are with how the end product looks. Imitation has two advantages:
  1. It gives the child the best chance to write the letter.
  2. It teaches the child the correct motor habits.

We are convinced that imitation has been neglected and should be rediscovered with appreciation.

Communicate: Share helpful secrets with others. If you want to help a child with handwriting, the best thing you can do is to get everyone on the same page. As long as everyone knows what is needed, you can move the remediation along. Use the Handwriting All Year ideas on page 160 to send mini homework assignments home. This unique program uses carefully created worksheets to facilitate grown-up demonstration and the child's imitation of letters and numbers.

Consistency and Follow-Through: Identify the problems, set up the team, and let the progress begin. If you are consistent, you will see progress in the child's handwriting.

Help Others: You may develop a love for helping children with handwriting. With HWT workshop training and the HWT program, you can become an HWT Level I Certified. Visit www.hwtcertification.com.

STRATEGIES FOR A PHYSICAL APPROACH

Handedness

By the time formal handwriting training begins, it's important for a child to have developed hand dominance. Sometimes you have to help the child choose the more skilled hand and then facilitate use of that hand. Collaborate with parents, teachers, therapists, and other significant individuals in the child's life to determine the more skilled hand. Create a checklist of activities for everyone to observe (brushing teeth, eating, dressing, cutting, etc.) Together, you can position materials on the preferred side, and encourage use of the most skilled hand for handwriting.

Pencil Grip

Demonstration

Always demonstrate the correct hold and finger positions. Use the Pencil Pick-Up activity on page 78 in this guide and sing the *Picking Up My Pencil* song, Track 9, on the *Rock, Rap, Tap & Learn* CD.

Correct pencil grip in three easy steps

You can help a child develop a correct pencil grip or fix one that is awkward. The trick is that you don't teach grip by itself. Teach grip in three stages, and you will be impressed with how easy it becomes. The technique takes consistency and a little time. (See page 64 for an illustration of correct grips.) Tell students that you are going to show them a new way to hold their pencil, but that they are not yet allowed to use the new grip for their writing.

1. Pick-Up—Have the child pick up the pencil and hold it in the air with the fingers and thumb correctly placed. Help position the child's fingers if necessary. Tell your students, "Wow, that is a perfect pencil grip. Now make a few circles in the air with the perfect pencil grip. Drop it and do it again." Repeat this five times a day for a couple of weeks.

2. Scribble-Wiggle—Give students a piece of paper with five randomly placed dots. Have them pick up a pencil, hold it correctly, and put the pencil point on the dot. The little finger side of the pencil hand rests on the paper. Students make wiggly marks through and around the dot without lifting their pencils or hands. The helping hand is flat and holds the paper. The advantage of this step is that children develop their pencil grip and finger control without being critical of how the writing looks. Do this daily for a couple weeks.

3. Write—Have students pick up a pencil, hold it correctly, and write the first letter of their names. Add letters until the children can write their names easily with the correct grip. Once they are writing letters with their new grip, grant them permission to use it for all their writing.

Drive the Pencil Trick

(This is a summary of a tip from Betsy Daniel, COTA/L and Christine Bradshaw, OTR/L.) Name the fingers: The thumb is the dad, and the index finger is the mom. The remaining fingers are the child and any brothers, sisters, friends, or

pets. Say the pencil is the car. Just as in a real car, dad and mom sit in front and the kids, friends, or pets sit in back. For safe driving, dad shouldn't sit on mom's lap (thumb on top of index finger), and mom never sits on dad's lap (index finger on top of thumb)! If children use an overlapping or tucked-in thumb, remind them that no one can sit on anyone's lap while driving!

Adaptive Devices

If a child continues to have difficulty holding the pencil, there are a variety of grips available at school supply stores, art/stationary stores, and catalogs. Their usefulness varies from grip-to-grip and child-to-child. Experiment with them, and use them only if they make it easier for the child to hold the pencil correctly. With young children, physical devices should not be used as substitutes for physical demonstration.

Rubber Band Trick: Check the angle of the pencil. If it's standing straight up, the pencil will be difficult to hold and will cause tension in the fingertips. Put a rubber band around the child's wrist. Loop another rubber band to the first one. Pull the loop over the pencil eraser. This may keep the pencil pulled back at the correct angle. You may make or buy a more comfortable version that uses ponytail holders.

Reward a Grip

Sometimes young children need motivation to use their new grip. You can offer them a small reward for remembering how to hold their pencils correctly. Track their progress so they can see how close they are to reaching their reward. Attach a photo of their correct pencil grip with a small strip of paper to their desks and stamp them every time you catch them holding their pencil correctly. Thus you help them build a good motor pattern.

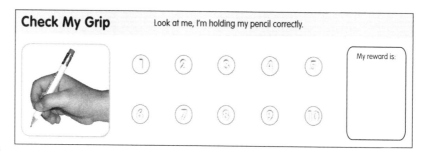

Pencil Pressure

Sometimes children have to learn to judge and moderate their pencil pressure. It's more common for a child to push too hard than not hard enough. Regardless, both can cause problems.

    Too hard: Try a mechanical pencil so the child has to control the amount of pressure. You can also have children place paper on a mouse pad (if they press too hard they will poke holes in their paper). *

    Too soft: Have the child pencil in small shapes until they are black. Use pencils with softer lead.

*Suggestions should be tried at home before they're used at school, because remedies for pencil pressure problems can be frustrating to the child.

Posture

Children will sacrifice all stability for mobility. They love to move! Children need to sit in their chairs with their hips, knees, and feet at a 90-degree angle. Check the furniture size. The chair and desk should fit the child. If you can't find a smaller chair, place something (a phone book, box, etc.) under the child's feet for stability. This will help them to sit up when it's time to write.

Helper Hand

Where is the helping hand; the hand that isn't holding the pencil? We've all seen helping hands in laps, twirling hair, or propping up foreheads. You can nag the child, but you'll get better results if you talk directly to the hand! Try it! Take the child's helping hand in yours and pretend to talk to that hand.

Name the helping hand. For example: Ask John what other name he likes that starts with **J**. If John says "Jeremy," tell him that you are going to name his helping hand "Jeremy." Have a little talk with Jeremy, the helping hand. Tell Jeremy that he's supposed to help by holding the paper. Say that John is working really hard on his handwriting, but he needs Jeremy's help. Show Jeremy where he's supposed to be. Tell John that he might have to remind Jeremy about his job.

Kids think this is a hoot. They don't get embarrassed because it's the helping hand, not them, that is being corrected. It's not John who needs to improve, it's Jeremy. This is a face-saving, but effective, reminder. Flat fingers please! A flat (but not stiff) helping hand promotes relaxed writing. Put your hand flat on the table and try to feel tension—there isn't any! Make a fist and feel the tension! Children can get uptight while writing, but a flat helping hand decreases tension.

STRATEGIES FOR SELF-CORRECTION

Sometimes children are fine with handwriting but they over- or under-correct their work. To help with this, you can download The Eraser Challenge and Spot Good Writing at **www.hwtears.com/click**.

The Eraser Challenge

Some children spend a lot of time erasing. Those who erase often will tend to be slow and lag behind in their work. If you want to control the amount of erasing without taking away erasers, strike a deal using the following strategy:

1. Download the Eraser Flags.
2. Tape them to your students' desks or send them home for parents to use when helping with homework.
3. Every time children erase, they pull a flag.
4. Play a game by challenging children to have a certain amount of flags left at the end of the day.

The Eraser Challenge	How many erasers will you have left at the end of the day?

1 2 3 4 5 6 7 8 9 10

Spot Good Writing

Some children have good handwriting skills but don't carry them over into general school work. Make your expectations clear and make children accountable. Download and print these notes to help children improve what's good and what's not.

SPOT GOOD WRITING

Can you check all of these?
☐ Strokes - start, sequence of letters good
☐ Sit letters on line
☐ Size of letters seems suitable
☐ Spaces in sentences
☐ Start with a CAPITAL
☐ Stop with a ? !
☐ See if others can read

Handwriting Without Tears®   © 2008 Jan Z. Olsen

Spacing

Teach your students to put letters in a word close to each other. Have them put their index fingers up and bring them close together, without touching. Tell them, "In a word, the letters are close, but don't touch." Draw fingers for them.

Sentence Spacing with Pennies

Give your children pennies or chips to use. Teach them how to look at a short simple sentence and fix the pennies to match as in this example.

I   SEE   A   DOG.

Sick Sentence Clinic

The teacher writes a sentence with the letters too far apart. Circle each word in the sentence. Now copy the sentence over, putting the letters closer. For example:

I a m b i g.   I am big.

Now, write a sentence with the letters too close. Children underline each word in the sentence. Leave space between words. Now copy the sentence over with spaces between the words.

Icanrun.   I can run.

The Nothing Bottle

If students run their words together:

Say that you will give them what they need for spaces. Have them hold out their hands to catch it. Take a huge empty bottle (or any container) and make a big show of pouring into their hands. Ask, "What did you get?" Nothing! Tell them to put nothing after every word they write.

Nothing Bottle

STRATEGIES FOR PRINTING SKILLS

Memory
- Play visual memory games with capital and lowercase flashcards.
- Use HWT readiness materials (Wood Pieces Set, Capital Letter Cards, Stamp and See Screen) with the *Pre-K Teacher's Guide* and *Kindergarten Teacher's Guide*.
- Go on letter scavenger hunts. Look for things around the school or house that begin with letters that need to be practiced.
- Build a letter card repertoire. Start with just the letters that the child can name instantly. Add one new letter at a time.

Orientation
- Correct number reversals by choosing one reversal per assignment. If children reverse many of their numbers, work on them one at a time beginning with the lowest number. Master that formation before moving on to another number.
- Use Wet–Dry–Try. The Slate Chalkboard works for capitals and number reversals; the Blackboard with Double Lines is for lowercase. See page 46 of this guide.
- Play the Mystery Letter game using Gray Blocks or Slate.

Placement
- Teach bumping the lines using the Blackboard with Double Lines and Wet–Dry–Try. See page 48 of this guide.
- Mark scores on a baseline.
- Do demonstration/imitation of small, tall, descending letter placement.
- Do letter sizes, page 54 of this guide, followed by writing letters or words on double lines.
- Model how different paper is used and how letters sit on the lines.

Size
- Use paper that promotes an age–appropriate letter size.
- Avoid poorly designed worksheets: overly busy, confusing lines, inadequate room for writing.
- Use landscape rather than portrait worksheets.

Start/Sequence
- Demonstrate/imitate to build correct habits for letters.
- Teach the TOP! See page 19 of this guide.
- Use ☺ cue to help children notice the top left corner.
- Use Slate Chalkboard with Wet–Dry–Try, page 46 of this guide.
- Use Gray Block Paper.

Spacing
- Teach spacing actively.
- Use worksheets that model generous spacing: horizontal, landscape format if possible.
- Use the *Sentence Song* on the *Rock, Rap, Tap & Learn* CD, Track 7.
- Use Sentence Spacing with Pennies, page 158 of this guide.
- Teach children about spacing using their fingers, page 158 of this guide.
- Teach the Sick Sentence Clinic, page 158 of this guide.
- Use the Nothing Bottle Activity, page 158 of this guide.

Control
- Correct children's other printing skills to help improve their control.
- Turn to the next page for tips if you suspect the teaching method has caused problems with control.
- Consult an occupational therapist if you suspect that control is affected by a fine motor problem (clue: all other skills are okay, but control is poor).

STRATEGIES FOR OTHER METHODS AND HOME PRACTICE

Other Methods

Children in your classroom may have learned other styles of handwriting. Support and accept other styles, but only if they work. If a particular style is giving a child problems with speed or neatness, you will have to decide whether to modify or reteach it.

Typically, scripted print is something that can be modified. For example, you can teach children to eliminate unnecessary tails on letters that may be causing problems. You can even take away the slant.

hat **hall**

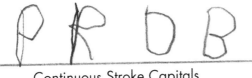 

If the style is delaying the child's academics, then it might be in the child's best interest to re-teach. For example, children often will make capitals with a continuous stroke. If they can't retrace well or stay on the line, you may need to re-teach the letter using a more developmentally appropriate approach.

Continuous Stroke Capitals

Re-taught using HWT Frog Jump Strategies

Handwriting All Year

What do you do when the workbook is complete? You continue with short lessons to maintain and improve printing skills. You might like to follow a weekly routine. We have ideas for every day of the week. Here are just a few:

Monday: Capital Letters Try a Capital – Country activity.
Have children write the name of a country that begins with the first letter of their name.

Tuesday: Lowercase Letters
Sing *Descending Letters*, track 19, on the *Rock, Rap, Tap & Learn* CD. Write words with **g j y p** or **q**.

Wednesday: Words
Learn some Greek and Latin words. Write the word, the English meaning, and an English word that uses the Latin/Greek word. For example: port = carry → portable

Thursday: Sentences
Write Subject – Verb sentences. Display a group of subject words and a group of verb words from your word wall. Let children make up their own sentences. Remind them about capitals, spacing, and ending punctuation.

Friday: Fun and Numbers
Use silly fill-in-the-blank stories. Read each other's or do them together.

EXTRAS

Here we include a few final things to facilitate good handwriting instruction.

Report Card Insert

Some report cards don't have a place to grade or mark handwriting success. This is particularly important in the lower grades because handwriting performance can affect other academic subjects. If your report card doesn't allow space for handwriting, use this downloadable form and include it with your students' report cards. It will demonstrate that you value handwriting and are monitoring progress.

Handwriting Report	Name				
Printing Skill	**Q1**	**Q2**	**Q3**	**Q4**	**Comments**
Forms capitals correctly					
Forms lowercase correctly					
Forms numbers correctly					
Writes on lines					
Writes appropriate size					
Applies skills					

Educating Others

Because handwriting often takes a back seat in today's elementary schools, it's wonderful for someone knowledgeable in handwriting, specifically the Handwriting Without Tears® method, to step forward and share that knowledge with others. Whether you are educating parents at a back-to-school night or presenting in front of a language arts committee, the information you share will improve the likelihood that others will recognize the importance of teaching handwriting.

Parents

Educate parents about HWT, pencil grip, and printing skills. Giving parents letter/number charts at the start of school helps them understand how to form letters and help their child at home. You can find parent articles to print and distribute on the website.

Colleagues

Share your HWT knowledge with your friends and co-workers. If you have attended or plan to attend our workshops, tell friends about it, or—better yet—invite them to come along. Often, all it takes is one teacher from a school getting excited about handwriting to inspire an entire school to learn more.

Administrators and Committees

Principals can be your biggest advocates. Share the information you have learned with principals and other administrators. Discuss the benefits of handwriting consistency and how HWT can help. Many HWT advocates have successfully written proposals, initiated handwriting pilot studies, presented to language arts committees, and seen large districts adopt HWT district-wide. Email or call us for help: janolsen@hwtears.com or 301-263-2700. We will send you a CD loaded with everything you need to help others understand that handwriting should be an easy victory for children and how using Handwriting Without Tears® enables that success.

Teaching Guidelines

The HWT curriculum is highly adaptable and can be used in a number of ways. If you are looking for a completely structured approach, we created these guidelines to help you along. For faster-paced instruction skip review.*

Week	Monday	Tuesday	Wednesday	Thursday	Friday	Friday Numbers (during Math)
1 Pre-writing	**Wood Pieces Activities** TGK pg. 33-43	**Shake Hands with Me** TGK pg. 18	**Wood Pieces Activities** TGK pg. 33-43	**Posture & Paper** TGK pg. 60-62 **Grip** TGK pg. 63-65	**Wood Pieces Activities** TGK pg. 33-43	
2 Pre-writing & Capitals	**Sign-In Please** TGK pg. 20	**Mat Man** TGK pg. 44 **Posture & Grip** TGK pg. 60-65	**Wood Pieces Activities** TGK pg. 33-43	**F** TGK pg. 79-80	**F in Gray Blocks** LN pg. 9	
3	**E** TGK pg. 81	**E in Gray Blocks** LN pg. 10	**D** TGK pg. 82	**D in Gray Blocks** LN pg. 11	**Sign-In Please** TGK pg. 20 **Grip** TGK pg. 63-65	**Number 1** TGK pg. 148 LN pg. 84
4	**P** TGK pg. 83	**P in Gray Blocks** LN pg. 12	**B** TGK pg. 84	**B in Gray Blocks** LN pg. 13	**Posture & Paper** TGK pg. 60-62 **Grip** TGK pg. 63-65	**Number 2** TGK pg. 148 LN pg. 85
5	**R** TGK pg. 85	**R in Gray Blocks** LN pg. 14	**N** TGK pg. 86	**N in Gray Blocks** LN pg. 15	***Review Capitals** F E D P B R N	**Number 3** TGK pg. 149 LN pg. 86
6	**M** TGK pg. 87	**M in Gray Blocks** LN pg. 16	***Review Frog Jump Capitals**	**Mystery Letter Game** TGK pg. 88 LN pg. 17	**Mystery Letter Game** TGK pg. 88 LN pg. 17	**Number 4** TGK pg. 149 LN pg. 87
7	**H** TGK pg. 89	**H in Gray Blocks** LN pg. 18	**K** TGK pg. 90	**K in Gray Blocks** LN pg. 19	**L** TGK pg. 91	**Number 5** TGK pg. 150 LN pg. 88
8	**L in Gray Blocks** LN pg. 20	**U** TGK pg. 92	**U in Gray Blocks** LN pg. 21	**V** TGK pg. 93	**V in Gray Blocks** LN pg. 22	**Number 6** TGK pg. 150 LN pg. 89
9	**W** TGK pg. 94	**W in Gray Blocks** LN pg. 23	**X** TGK pg. 95	**X in Gray Blocks** LN pg. 24	**Y** TGK pg. 96	**Number 7** TGK pg. 151 LN pg. 90
10	**Y in Gray Blocks** LN pg. 25	**Z** TGK pg. 97	**Z in Gray Blocks** LN pg. 26	***Review Starting Corner Capitals**	**Words for Me** TGK pg. 98 LN pg. 27	**Number 8** TGK pg. 151 LN pg. 91
11	**C** TGK pg. 99	**C in Gray Blocks** LN pg. 28	**O** TGK pg. 100	**O in Gray Blocks** LN pg. 29	**Q** TGK pg. 101	**Number 9** TGK pg. 152 LN pg. 92
12	**Q in Gray Blocks** LN pg. 30	**G** TGK pg. 102	**G in Gray Blocks** LN pg. 31	**Mystery Letter Game** TGK pg. 103 LN pg. 32	**S** TGK pg. 104	**Number 10** TGK pg. 152 LN pg. 93
13	**S in Gray Blocks** LN pg. 33	**A** TGK pg. 105	**A in Gray Blocks** LN pg. 34	**I** TGK pg. 106	**I in Gray Blocks** LN pg. 35	**Numbers for Me** TGK pg. 153 LN pg. 94
14	**T** TGK pg. 107	**T in Gray Blocks** LN pg. 36	**J** TGK pg. 108	**J in Gray Blocks** LN pg. 37	**Words for Me** TGK pg. 109 LN pg. 38	***Review Numbers**

Week	Monday	Tuesday	Wednesday	Thursday	Friday
15 Capital Review	*Review Frog Jump Capitals	*Review Corner Start Capitals	*Review Center Starting Capitals	*Review Numbers	*Use Gray Block Paper to Review Capitals
16 Lowercase	c o TGK pg. 110-111	c o on Double Lines LN pg. 40-41	s TGK pg. 112	s on Double Lines LN pg. 42	Words with s TGK pg. 113 LN pg. 43
17	v TGK pg. 114	v on Double Lines LN pg. 44	w TGK pg. 115	w on Double Lines LN pg. 45	*Review Numbers
18	t TGK pg. 116	t on Double Lines LN pg. 46	Words for Me TGK pg. 116 LN pg. 47	*Review lowercase c o s v w t	*Review Numbers
19	a TGK pg. 118	a on Double Lines LN pg. 48	d TGK pg. 119	d on Double Lines LN pg. 49	g TGK pg. 120
20	g on Double Lines LN pg. 50	Sentences for Me TGK pg. 120 LN pg. 51	*Review lowercase a d g	u TGK pg. 121	u on Double Lines LN pg. 52
21	Words for Me TGK pg. 121 LN pg. 53	i TGK pg. 122	i on Double Lines LN pg. 54	e TGK pg. 123	e on Double Lines LN pg. 55
22	l TGK pg. 124	l on Double Lines LN pg. 56	Words for Me TGK pg. 124 LN pg. 57	k TGK pg. 125	k on Double Lines LN pg. 58
23	Words for Me TGK pg. 125 LN pg. 59	y TGK pg. 126	y on Double Lines LN pg. 60	j TGK pg. 127	j on Double Lines LN pg. 61
24 Review Week	*Review Capitals	*Review Numbers	*Review lowercase c o s v w t	*Review lowercase a d g	*Review lowercase u i e l k y j
25	p TGK pg. 129	p on Double Lines LN pg. 62	Words for Me TGK pg. 129 LN pg. 63	r TGK pg. 130	r on Double Lines LN pg. 64
26	n TGK pg. 131	n on Double Lines LN pg. 65	m TGK pg. 132	m on Double Lines LN pg. 66	Words for Me TGK pg. 132 LN pg. 67
27	h TGK pg. 133	h on Double Lines LN pg. 68	b TGK pg. 134	b on Double Lines LN pg. 69	*Review lowercase p r n m h b
28	f TGK pg. 135	f on Double Lines LN pg. 70	Words for Me TGK pg. 135 LN pg. 71	q TGK pg. 136	q on Double Lines LN pg. 72
29	x TGK pg. 137	x on Double Lines LN pg. 73	z TGK pg. 138	z on Double Lines LN pg. 74	Words for Me TGK pg. 138 LN pg. 75
Weeks to Follow	*Review Capitals	Activity Pages	*Review Lowercase Letters	Activity Pages	*Review Numbers

FAQs

Why aren't there grade levels on your workbooks?
In some instances, we recommend that an older child be taught using a workbook from a lower grade. We don't want the child to feel bad, so we remove the grade label. Thus we focus on the skill level, not the grade level.

Why don't you use Wood Pieces to make J or U?
All the capital letters except **J** and **U** can be made very well with the Wood Pieces. **J** and **U** are awkward because when made with Wood Pieces they end up disproportionate relative to the other capitals. Further, **J** and **U** are written with a continuous fluid stroke and to do them with Wood Pieces requires breaking that up, 2 pieces for **J** and 3 pieces for **U**. Also, the Slate works beautifully for teaching these letters. Feel free to make **J** or **U** with Wood Pieces for fun activities like trying to write the child's name with Wood Pieces.

Do you ever use Wood Pieces for numbers?
We love the Slate for teaching numbers but the Wood Pieces work well for teaching numbers **1** to **5** and **7** and **0**. The others **6**, **8** and **9** end up looking a little strange and don't really represent the way those numbers are written.

Why do you sometimes use a y for a Y and an I for an I?
One is informational, one is instructional. When we teach the letter for handwriting, we want to be sure that the letter is representative of the easiest way to form it. Typically, the other form is used in sentences that will be read, not written. We often use non-HWT forms in our teacher's guides.

The Gray Blocks on the capital practice seem to fade out. Is this true?
Yes, we progressively lighten the shading on the Gray Block. Children in elementary school are asked to write on a huge variety of line styles. We use Gray Blocks and HWT Double Lines as a means of helping children develop an independent sense of how letters are placed. After some instruction and practice, this enables children to be successful on all styles of lines (or no lines). The fading Gray Block is just one step in the process of building the child's ability to write letters the correct size and put them in the right spot.

Why don't you teach capitals with a continuous stroke?
When children are young, their motor control is in a constant state of development. Therefore, having them trace back up a line in the initial stages of handwriting can lead to poor letter formation. We can get away with non-retrace of capitals because they are not used as frequently as the lowercase. However, when we move to lowercase, a retrace makes writing faster. We use the skills we develop in capitals to help children at the appropriate time.

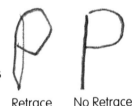

Retrace   No Retrace

Why do you assign multisensory assignments to each letter? Can't you use them interchangeably?
We assign them to help you spread them out throughout your teaching strategies. If you have one that is your favorite or your classes favorite by all means use what is popular. Don't stop there, you might even create a few of your own!

Why are some of your words are so short?
The words are CVC words: words that have a consonant-vowel-consonant pattern. They are good for young children who are just learning to read and write.

Why didn't you include x, y, and z when teaching the first group of lowercase letters that are same as capitals?
Letters **x**, **y**, and **z** are used infrequently and have diagonals. We save them until the end because they are more difficult to form and not frequently used.

Why don't you start 6 in the center?
If you teach **b** in the starting corner children won't reverse it. Once children learn **b** they will naturally add a curve to the top. You shouldn't worry about **b** resembling a **b**—it won't last long.

Why don't you teach q and o with Magic C letters?
The letter **o** is a frequently used letter. We wanted to include it in the first group we taught. Letter **q** is an infrequently used letter and can be confused with **g**, so we save it for the end. When teaching **q** or reviewing lowercase, you may consider those letters as part of the Magic c letter group.

Lowercase Letter Frequency Chart

In 1948, Dr. Edward Dolch published a list of 220 high frequency words. He had word lists for preprimer, primer, first, second, and third grade. To identify high frequency printed words for grades K - 2, we used the 177 words on the lists through 2nd grade. Then, we counted how often each letter appears to determine individual letter frequency. This chart shows the letters in order of decreasing frequency. This information was helpful to us in planning our teaching order. Teachers can use this chart to make priority decisions about correcting or reviewing letters.

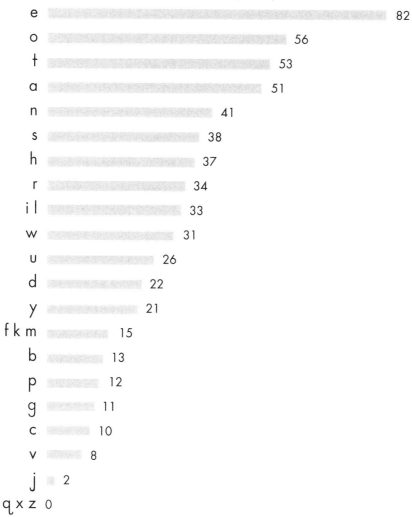

Letter	Frequency
e	82
o	56
t	53
a	51
n	41
s	38
h	37
r	34
i l	33
w	31
u	26
d	22
y	21
f k m	15
b	13
p	12
g	11
c	10
v	8
j	2
q x z	0

The Top 40 Words

Mastering frequently used words is important for fluency. Use this list from the Dolch sight words for practice and review. Be sure to avoid words that use letters you haven't taught yet.

1. the	11. his	21. with	31. be
2. to	12. that	22. up	32. have
3. and	13. she	23. all	33. go
4. he	14. for	24. look	34. we
5. you	15. on	25. is	35. am
6. it	16. they	26. her	36. then
7. of	17. but	27. there	37. little
8. in	18. had	28. some	38. down
9. was	19. at	29. out	39. do
10. said	20. him	30. as	40. can

Capitals, Lowercase Letters, and Numbers